STAND UP AND BE COUNTED

Here Tony Campolo, activist extraordinary and visionary motivator, opens his mind and heart on aspects of spiritual renewal . . . Perceiving that true revival has feet, he maps out paths of neighbour-love along which quickened Christians should be walking today. One need not agree with all his opinions to find profound instruction and challenge in these pages.

— JAMES PACKER, author of *Knowing God*

Keen analysis coupled with solid remedy — that is the remarkable combination which Campolo offers Christ's people in this book. Nothing I have read matches it in inspiration and instruction.

— DAVID HUBBARD, president, Fuller Theological Seminary

I used to pray that God would mellow Tony. Now I pray that God will *move me* — and He often does through Tony's books and this is one of them!

— BILL HYBELS, senior pastor of Willow Creek Community Church

A powerful plea to transcend cultural Christianity and embrace costly discipleship. Classic Campolo — provocative, probing, powerful.

— RON SIDER, executive director, Evangelicals for Social Action, and professor of Theology & Culture, Eastern Baptist Theological Seminary

A powerful, prophetic message for the 1990s. A must-read for all followers of Jesus.

— RUTH A. TUCKER, visiting professor at Trinity Evangelical Divinity School

Tony Campolo is too funny to fit the usual stereotypes of a prophet. But he certainly says prophetic things that the Church needs to listen to. And in this book he takes the further, more difficult step of pointing to examples of people who are doing it right.

— PHILIP YANCEY, author of *Disappointment With God*

Stand Up and Be Counted

How to change the world for good

Tony Campolo

MarshallPickering
An Imprint of HarperCollinsPublishers

Marshall Pickering is an Imprint of
HarperCollins*Religious*
Part of HarperCollins*Publishers*
77–85 Fulham Palace Road, London W6 8JB

Originally published in the United States of America
in 1991 by HarperSanFrancisco,
a division of HarperCollins*Publishers* Ltd,
under the title *Wake Up America!*

First published in Great Britain
in 1993 by Marshall Pickering

1 3 5 7 9 10 8 6 4 2

Grateful acknowledgement is made for use of the following:
"Class of '57" by Harold Reid and Don Reid, © 1972 by House of Cash, Inc. (BMI).
Administered by CMI, Nashville, TN. All rights reserved. Used by permission. "How
Great Thou Art", © 1953 by Manna Music, Inc. International copyright secured. All
rights reserved. Used by permission.

All Scripture quotations in this publication are from the Holy Bible,
Authorized Version.

Adapted for publication in Great Britain by James Tweed

Tony Campolo asserts the moral right to be
identified as the author of this work

A catalogue record for this book is
available from the British Library

ISBN 0 551 02794 0

Set in Galliard by Avocet Typesetters, Bicester, Oxon

Printed and bound in Great Britain by
HarperCollinsManufacturing Glasgow

To Dick Lane
A model for those who want to know
what a great Christian looks like

Contents

Preface

This has been a hard book to write because it is filled with emotion. My future and the future of my country are wrapped up in its message. As I wrote it, I was forced to endure painful examination of both myself and the other people on this planet that I call my own. What I discovered is that I am part of a dying culture and of a people who have lost their dreams and visions.

But this is also a book filled with hope. I believe that a new breed of Christians with a new way of influencing the world is coming to centre stage. And this new breed of Christians, I am convinced, is going to breathe new life into those dry bones called the West.

No earthly being needs to give birth to this movement of renewal. The Lord Himself is making it happen. The Kingdom is already among us as mustard seeds, and soon the fruit will be evident. It will not come in violent revolutions, which, in the end, do little except to change the palace guard. It will not come from political action that is designed to change things from the top down. Instead, it will come from a new breed of Christians working locally in programmes and projects that separately and to the outside observer will not seem like much. But look again, because in what I call "mid-range" activities, a new society will begin to flex its muscles and it will get up and walk around.

But before I get into my story, let me acknowledge the

people who helped me get it together and into print. There is Mary Noel Keough, who made sure the manuscript got edited and typed. And there are Amy Kay Watson and Patricia Carroll, who actually did a lot of the typing. There is Lonnie Hull, the editor from HarperSanFrancisco who made me rethink what I had to say and how I would say it. And then there is the real partner in this mission – Peggy, my wife. People always ask, "Do you really write all of those books?" The answer is, "No! She does!" At least she sees to it that they get written right.

– *Tony Campolo*

Introduction

Late one afternoon I received a phone call from my friend John Bernbaum of the Christian College Coalition. He told me that a group of top educators from the Soviet Union was coming to the United States. The group included the rectors of two of the most prestigious universities of the USSR as well as the Russian Deputy Minister of Education. John explained that they were interested in seeing the things religious groups here in the United States are doing in the way of social service. Since I head an organization that has a variety of inner-city ministries in the greater Philadelphia area, John thought it would be a good thing for these Russians to see our work. I was pleased to have the opportunity to show off what my staff was accomplishing, so I readily agreed to the visit.

When the Russians arrived, they seemed impressed. With great enthusiasm I took them to our various latchkey programmes which take care of children after school hours. I showed off our youth clubs and explained how we communicate Christian values to ghetto teenagers. Finally, I took them to a special Christian school that we have established for disadvantaged children.

Everywhere these Russian visitors went they interviewed people – children and young people as well as adults. Their questions were probing and astute. They listened with intensity and they took copious notes.

At the end of the day we had a debriefing time, and I asked my guests about the impressions they had gained from the day's experiences. Their responses surprised me. "These teenagers are so materialistic!" was one response. Another added, "All that these young people talked about was making money." But the most unexpected answer came from the Deputy Minister of Education, who reluctantly remarked, "I am somewhat disappointed in your children. Since they are Christians, I expected that they would be concerned about spiritual things. Instead, they are more materialistic than the Marxist youth in my country. They seem to be devoid of any lofty, idealistic vision."

These responses were not what I had expected to hear. Seeing "Christian" children through the eyes of people from other countries provided something of a surprise, especially in light of the fact that these people who had pointed out the materialism of our youth were Marxists.

I asked myself if Christian kids in America have always been this way, or if this evident materialism and lack of spirituality is a recent development. I wondered if I had been like these kids when I was a teenager, or if something had died in the psyche of youth since those days. And I asked myself if only young people were this way, or if all of us had changed during the last few decades.

Has the spirit of idealism departed from our collective consciousness without our being aware of it? Can it be that, in an era when religion has become one of the most prominent features of our culture, we have lost our guiding inner light and lofty calling? And if we have become a people of dry bones, can these dry bones ever rise up and walk again?

This book is about such questions. Together, I want us to talk about the spiritual condition of the West and to examine what has been happening to us over the last few decades. As you might surmise from the tone of these opening paragraphs,

I do not think that the diagnosis will be good. I have to admit that I sense that something has been lost. I have a feeling that sacredness has been "slip slidin' away".

But there is something else we must look at. There is a strange and mysterious force at work in our world. I can feel it, and most people with whom I talk can feel it too. It is a force that evidences itself in subtle ways in the music on Broadway and in the paintings of Andrew Wyeth. It is an intangible reality that lies just beneath the surface of the yuppie consciousness and is waiting to be born.

This force is nothing less than a spirit that will give birth to a new and different West with a new and different faith. It has a dynamism that has the wherewithal to sweep away the encroaching lethargy that seems to beset us on every side. It has an idealism that can counteract the cynicism eating away at our collective soul. It is a spirit that, in the words of the apostle Paul, is "with us, and in us," struggling to take form and to fan the dying embers of Western nations back to life again. It is a spirit that will overcome the feeling that we are living at the beginning of the end and will make us believe that, in reality, we are facing a new beginning.

This book is not only about what we have lost. It is also about the "new thing" God is doing in our midst, and it is an invitation for you to be a part of it. It is about the rebirth of a red-hot movement of the spirit that stands against the cold death wish that hitherto has haunted our souls and generated anxiety about our future. I hope you will come away from reading this book convinced that God has not given up on our culture and that he is even now calling you to join Him in making our society radically new.

Chapter 1

How Did We Get So Good at Being So Bad?

This is not the first book to begin with the famous Dickens quote, "It was the best of times; it was the worst of times." But few quotes so aptly describe the end of the twentieth century. It is a time of brilliant technological achievement; but it also is a time when technology has overwhelmed us with problems. It is a time when it has at last become possible to produce enough food for everyone on the planet; but it also is a time when political and economic barriers have prevented food from getting to millions who live on the verge of starvation. It is a time when "the good life" seems within the grasp of so many; and yet it is a time when more people live in a narcissistic hell than most of us can imagine.

For those of us who live in the Western nations, the end of the twentieth century has been a time of triumph. Our political philosophy has swept away its opposition. The liberal democratic ideals born out of the Enlightenment and tested in the crucibles of the American and French Revolutions have won out over the threats of fascism on the one hand and communism on the other, and the values of Western democracy have become an ideal for the entire world.

The "victory" of Western capitalism in America has come from neither military conquest nor rational debate. Instead, it has come from something much less dramatic or noble. It has triumphed by virtue of the fact that its socioeconomic system has produced more consumer goods than any other.

Consequently, the West's way of life has apparently become not only the most desirable in the world but appears, to most people, the only viable one. In the end, it is because democratic capitalism has produced more things for more people than any of its competitors that its reign has gained sway over the minds of most of humanity. It has delivered more decent housing, more cars, more home appliances, more designer jeans, more television sets, and more gourmet foods than anyone had hitherto dreamed possible.

Living in the "free world" has become synonymous with having consumer goods. This is what our system is all about. And when at last the hideous Berlin Wall came tumbling down, it was these consumer goods produced under the auspices of our social system that the people from the Eastern Bloc nations rushed in to grab. As one expatriate from East Germany so eloquently said, "We came! We saw! We shopped!" At the end of the twentieth century, democratic capitalism has created the greatest society of consumer goods ever known to the human race, and against that fact no ideological doctrine supporting an alternative system seems to stand a chance.

"It cannot be as simple as that," some will say. "People will not be satisfied with consumer goods alone. There must be deep spiritual reasons why democratic capitalism has won." Antimaterialistic pulpiteers rant on, claiming that if that is all there is to the triumph of our way of life, then it will not last. "People need homes, not just houses," they say. "They need love, not just things. They need meaning, not just entertainment."

Spiritual Gratification through Material Means

What the would-be spiritual oracles fail to understand about our "advanced" capitalist social system is that the means have been devised to make spiritual realities somewhat unreal to most of us. More accurately, ways have been found in our consumer-oriented society to reduce spiritual hungers to emotions that can be gratified by purchasing the things being sold to us through the mass media. The tension between the spiritual and the material spheres of life increasingly is being overcome. In the context of our new social order, we more and more are being led to believe that our deepest spiritual needs, the sorts of realities the Bible talks about, can be met simply by buying the right consumer goods.

If such assertions seem absurd, then consider how so many of the advertisements on television promise to deliver to us the blessings that, upon reflection, we once supposed could come only from the right relationships with God and with our neighbours. Consider how the popular media are now overcoming differences that once existed between the satisfactions provided by spiritual well-being and the satisfactions that come from consumer goods.

For instance, Coca-Cola (in what may be the most famous ad of all time) replicates the Biblical imagery of the Day of Pentecost. In the ad, people from various ethnic groups from around the world are assembled on a hilltop, holding hands and singing:

> I want to teach the world to sing
> in perfect harmony . . .

But what creates this perfect harmony for broken humanity, overcomes the curse of Babel, unifies us, and overcomes our sense of separateness is not the Holy Spirit. It's Coca-Cola! For much of the world, Coke has become "The Real Thing".

Or think how the intimacy of biblical *koinonia* (fellowship) apparently can be generated by buying the politically correct brand of beer. A recent advertisement based on the popular

Bill Forsyth film *Local Hero* illustrates this nicely. As in the film, an executive sent from a huge oil multinational lands by helicopter in a small, idyllic Scottish village with scale plans showing how it will be made into a refinery. However, on meeting the community in their local pub where he knocks back a pint of their finest, he grabs the plans, crumples them into a ball and throws them into the blazing log fire. Turning his back on big business, he acknowledges his new friends, real friends compared to the faceless people running the corporation and ruining the lives of those they have never – and will never – see.

The message is simple. A good beer puts the world to rights and breaks down the barriers of class, race and creed. As John Lennon sang: "And the world will live as one." However, I don't think the illusory one of advertising was what he had in mind.

In our TV ads, it is as though the ecstasy of the spirit experienced by a St Theresa or a St Francis can be reduced to the gratification coming from a particular car, and the kind of love that Christ compared to His love for His church can be expressed by buying the right kind of wristwatch "for that special person in your life". In all of this media hype, things are sold to us on the basis that our deepest emotional and psychological needs will be met by having the right consumer goods.

Hitherto, spiritual gratification could come only via spiritual means. Thus, people were urged to choose between the things of this world and the blessings of God. Now, that duality has been overcome. Ours is an age in which spiritual blessings are being promised to those who buy material things. The spiritual is being absorbed by the physical. The fruit of the spirit, suggests the media, can be had without God and without spiritual disciplines. It is not simply that we are materialists who crave the goods that flood our markets, but that we are now a people who subconsciously have been made to believe that in these things we will find an end to the spiritual longings at the ground of our being.

Perhaps the most evil consequence of selling consumer goods in this manner is that people like us no longer know what spiritual longings really are. We have become alienated from our real needs. Spiritual longings, which most of us can no longer even define, have come to be so identified with consumer goods that these consumer goods have taken on a quality of ultimateness for us.

But there is a catch in all of this. We sense that as the ads play up the theme of friendship, our loneliness becomes more acute. As the psychic ecstasy is played out on the electronic screen, our feelings of being hollow and empty become more severe. Those of us who long for love become more conscious of our plight as love seems to come so easily to those who buy the right things. These same processes are at work in ad themes ranging from self-worth to feeling free to define one's own destiny. The ads only increase our awareness of what is missing from our lives. They only heighten our consciousness of discontent.

When they have finished practising their magic on us, the ads are really capable only of getting us to spend our money, while leaving us estranged from ourselves. We think it is the things that we want. We have forgotten that the spiritual blessings that the ads have associated with the things are really the desires of our hearts.

You would think that sooner or later we would see through these not-too-subtle deceptions. But thirsty people want to believe in their mirages. We want the ads to be true. And wishes can keep deceptions alive for a long, long time.

Even when the things depicted in the ads fail to deliver what the ads promise, we do not grasp the nature of the deception. There are always *new* ads that tell us of *new* things that have just been invented. These new things, they claim, will give us the "full satisfaction" we crave, even if the things previously advertised left us disappointed. The new products, we are told, will really do the trick if we will just give them a try. And so we go on and on, buying more and more, and all the time feeling less and less satisfied with life.

How Necessary is the False Consciousness Created by Ads?

Is all of this psychological manipulation really necessary? Does our economy really require the spiritual deception that lies behind so much of what we see and hear through the media? Has it really become necessary for us to have our minds seduced by images of consumer goods that supposedly provide us with everything from peace of mind to loving relationships?

Unfortunately, the answer to all of these questions is, "Yes!" Without the ads we wouldn't buy what we have to buy to keep our Western economics going. The industrial machine has become so efficient that we are unable to purchase all the things it can produce. But if we are to keep people employed, that is exactly what we have to do. Buying home-produced goods is essential if we are to have jobs.

Unfortunately, (or fortunately; I am not convinced which) most people already have everything they need. At least that is true for those of us with money to spend. Those of us who do can think of little we need that we do not already have. We need no better evidence of that than Christmas, when our most serious problem is not how to get enough money to buy presents but what to buy for friends and relatives who have "everything".

When faced with the task of trying to get us to buy what we do not need in ever-increasing quantities, the advertising people are left with no alternative except to pretend that the things they are selling will meet spiritual and psychological needs. That is why the ads take the form that they do. That is why material consumer goods are sold to us on the basis that they will meet our deeply felt needs for community, friendship, sexual identity, self-worth, love, and peace of mind.

We ought to think twice before we condemn these Madison Avenue wizards who get us to buy what we do not need by soft-selling us to Saatchi-ration point. What would we do without them? Such absurdity is what our society is all about.

Enslavement to Alienation

Among the many side effects of the commercial process is, according to the late sociologist Herbert Marcuse, a tendency to think that the artificially created wants (i.e., consumer goods) generated by ads are more essential to our wellbeing than the meeting of the real needs that go with being human.

Marcuse went on to explain that this commercial system has so permeated our consciousness that we are now caught up in a comfortable, attractive, pleasant form of slavery. And it is the worst kind of slavery, because freedom from it becomes nearly impossible. We would never consider rebelling against a social system that gives us what we *think* we want.

When Phil and Cynthia got married they were sure they would create the perfect family. They had idyllic images of living in a cottage in the country, sitting with their children in front of a fireplace on Christmas Eve. They thought of the long walks and talks they would have, and the deep sense of sharing that would be theirs. Well, it didn't happen. And just after Christmas, Phil and Cynthia filed for a divorce. The disintegration of their marriage was the inevitable consequence of being enslaved to "the system".

At first, things had seemed to go well. Phil worked as an

insurance salesman and apparently made a decent living. Cynthia became a school teacher and very much enjoyed her work. But as the two of them tried to get themselves situated, it appeared to them that they needed more money than they were making between them. They just didn't seem to be able to buy all the things they thought they needed.

The problem seemed easy enough to solve. That was what Phil liked about selling insurance. If you needed more money, all you had to do was work a little harder, make a few extra calls on possible clients, and go to a few more sales conferences to improve your skills and to jack up motivation. There would be less time for those long walks and for the "sharings", but a guy's got to do what a guy's got to do. At least, that's what he told himself.

When the baby came, Phil and Cynthia were in a quandary. Of course they wanted the baby, but they also needed the money that came from Cynthia's teaching. The solution to the dilemma seemed to be child-care. Cynthia wouldn't be there to see little Jonathan take his first steps, and at times her little boy seemed to have more of a liking for his nanny than for her, but then one has to make sacrifices if one is to provide a child with the things he needs. At least, that's what she told herself.

As time slipped by, something died in their marriage. Phil was always too tired and always had too little time to empathize with Cynthia. Cynthia ended up doing most of the housework and became exhausted feeding a small child, putting him to bed, and, of course, shopping for all the things he needed. It was no wonder Phil and Cynthia always seemed a bit on edge and often gave curt answers to each other, but they had all the things they thought they needed. And besides, they were providing a good home for Jonathan. At least, that's what they told themselves.

This past Christmas things came to a head. Christmas has

a way of bringing out people's problems. I suppose it is because Christmas embodies so many memories of what used to be and calls forth recollections of what was hoped would be. Whatever the reasons, Christmas was such a hollow, empty day that it revealed what Phil and Cynthia long had suspected. Their marriage was not a marriage at all.

These are the consequences of the kinds of sacrifices people make in order to get the money they have to have to buy the things they don't need for people who have everything. This is the kind of unconscious slavery that Marcuse was talking about. Phil and Cynthia thought they were free, but they had been manipulated into enslavement to the things that "the system" had made ultimately important to them.

Yet it is in the throes of this time of triumph that the liberal democratic capitalistic society we have created faces its greatest threat and challenge. The threat is not posed by anything external. It is not a challenge that arises from the menace of some totalitarian dictator or belligerent nuclear power or the terrorism promoted by a few Muslim fanatics that jeopardize our golden age and our optimism about the future.

Something Has Died in the West

It is not just Phil and Cynthia that have got me worried. Something has happened to all of us spiritually. Putting it in Biblical language, it seems as though the West itself has lost its soul. Something about our collective psyche has died. Apathy and numbness appear to have crept into our shared consciousness. And no amount of flag waving, jingoistic preaching, or nationalistic crusading has the potential for resurrecting our fading *volksgeist* to life again.

We're tired. Our Western culture is sick, our politicians cynical, and meanwhile our countries reel like a drunken man. In America we have elected the first Democrat as President

since Jimmy Carter in 1976 in an attempt to stem the
economic and moral malaise the country is in. Before he was
elected President, journalist P. J. O'Rourke said to Bill
Clinton: "For fifty years people in both parties have been
saying, 'Bring me your problems, and I'll give you a solution.
Maybe a maximalist solution, maybe a minimalist solution,
but I'll bring you some kind of solution'." To which Clinton
replied: "But I think when we started doing that, most of
the problems we were talking about had solutions."

The inference is that now there are no solutions. And the
situation is no different in Great Britain, with a complacent
government seeming to shoot itself in both feet with every
move it makes. By putting free-market economics before
people for well over a decade, the government has created
a country with low inflation but soaring unemployment.
Livelihoods have been casually and flippantly sacrificed on
the altar of free enterprise.

When the government announced in October 1992 that
it intended to close over thirty coal pits, thereby putting
30,000 men out of work and another 130,000 on the dole
due to the knock-on effect, the nation was horrified. What
was seen as government mismanagement united the nation
and London saw the largest protest march since the Campaign
for Nuclear Disarmament rallies in the early 1980s. A chord
was struck in ordinary people, even loyal Conservatives, with
no political axe to grind, the length and breadth of the
country, and they marched to say: "Enough." And at the
front were the church leaders, most notably the Bishop of
Wakefield, the Rt Rev. Nigel McCulloch, who has carried
on a campaign despite the soundbite-sized spotlight of media
interest losing attention long before the situation was resolved.

If ever we want evidence that the love of money is the root
of all evil, we only have to look at the human cost of many
monetary policies and decisions. In seeking to gain the whole

world a government can lose its collective soul. But have we, too, been seduced by the same desires? Will we discover like Dr Faust, in Goethe's classic story, that what Mephistopheles offers, while attractive in the short term, costs our souls?

As I look around I see people scared to spend what money they have in the fear that they will lose their jobs and then their homes and then their marriages. The West is afraid of the future. In Germany racial hatred is on the increase because people are afraid. As I write three Turkish people, a grandmother and two children, have just been murdered in a firebomb attack in Hamburg by the ultra-right-wing German Nationalist Front.

Never have people had so much and been so afraid of losing it all. Perhaps because we have gained everything materially worth having, now our only *raison d'être* is to figure out how to hold onto it. Perhaps we have become a people who are frightened of having our hard-earned gains slip away from us. It is difficult to figure out just what the problem is. But I do know there is a problem. As a people we have become nervous and uncertain of ourselves. There is evidence that we have become afraid of our future.

Chapter 2

Is There a Prophet in the House?

When the new preacher came to town, everybody at the church was talking about how good he was and how much better he was than their old preacher. The town sceptic inquired with great interest of one of the deacons what this new man was preaching that made him so different from the old preacher.

"The old preacher told us we were all lost sinners and unless we repented we were all going to hell," was the answer.

"Well, what does this new preacher say?" the sceptic asked.

"This new preacher tells us we are all lost sinners and unless we repent we are all going to hell," was the reply.

"Well I'll be damned if I can tell the difference," was the sceptic's judgment.

"Oh there's a big difference," answered the deacon. "This one says it with tears in his eyes."

That, of course, is the mark of the true prophet. The true prophet makes his judgments and pronounces his warnings with tears in his eyes. Like Jeremiah, he weeps.

> Is there no balm in Gilead; is there no physician there? why then is not the health of the daughter of my people recovered?   Jeremiah 8:22

He knows that history will take its course and that, unless there is a real repentance, the people he loves and the nation to which he belongs will be no more. He grieves, "O earth, earth, earth . . ." (Jeremiah 22:29) because he knows that his people are dying and there is no future for the present order. With the true prophet there is weeping and gnashing of teeth.

We need a prophet like that today. We need more than a sociological critique explaining what is wrong with us and how we got this way. We need a prophet who will weep for us, who will stir us to a memory of what we were meant to be, who will reach into our collective consciousness and who will draw out of it the sorrowful memory of all we once aspired to be.

Such a prophet will not only weep floods of tears for us but also teach all of us to weep. And in that weeping lies our only hope, because it is the weeping that can break the numbness of our hearts and minds. It is the grieving that can teach us how to feel again. It is that weeping taught to us by the prophet that can break the mesmerizing spell of the deadly present and can show us how to be passionate again.

The Prophet as Dreamer

But weeping is only half of what the prophet will have to do. There is an even greater responsibility to be carried out. The task of the prophet is to nurture, nourish, and evoke a vision of an alternative to the dominant system. The prophet must generate hope for something that lies beyond the present order. We need a vision of an alternative future that will energize us and motivate us to act, a vision of possibilities that will make our blood run hot and give us the courage to revolt against the way things are.

A prophet's vision can replace people's numbness with energy. The possibility of a glorious "might be" can enable us to live in ways that appear dangerous to the custodians of the status quo. With vision, the dead bones can come alive. The psychically dead can be resurrected. The spiritual sleepers can be awakened. Out of sorrow for the death of the old can come a new dynamism to us; through the message of the prophet we can come to believe in a new heaven and a new earth. The apathy that works in people in dying societies can be dispelled. There can be passion. There can be a "new song" (Isaiah 42:10), and the fatigue that is so evident among those in the present order can be overcome:

> Hast thou not known? hast thou not heard, that the everlasting God, the LORD, the Creator of the ends of the earth, fainteth not, neither is weary? there is no searching of his understanding.
> He giveth power to the faint; and to them that have no might he increaseth strength.
> Even the youths shall faint and be weary, and the young men shall utterly fall:
> But they that wait upon the LORD shall renew their strength; they shall mount up with wings as eagles: they shall run, and not be weary; and they shall walk, and not faint. Isaiah 40:28–31

All of this energy comes from the message of the prophet. The people of the dying society can be "born again." The prophet's hope can generate the dynamism for change.

A Need for a Prophet in the Last Days

The West needs more than a patch-up job. Our sin goes deeper than anything that can be remedied with some improvements here and there. That is why the would-be prophets who preach at our religious convocations fail to measure up. Their messages may point out major flaws in our system and even call us to repentance, but something more is needed, something more profound and far-reaching. We need a voice crying in the wilderness of our consumer-oriented cultural system that will prepare the way of the Lord.

Who Might the Prophet Be?

Not too long ago I sat with some young people and reflected on the times in which we live. In the course of our discussions, I brought up our need for a prophet. I asked these young people to tell me what such a prophet might be like if God should raise one up today. I wanted to know which voice out of the historical past they thought we most needed to hear today. One suggestion was Martin Luther King. And I could see some justification for that suggestion.

For a little while, King's voice called us away from the deadness of our consumer-oriented way of life and challenged us to an idealism that is "not yet". What he said and how he said it almost shook us from our drowsiness. He almost made us believe that we have a higher calling and a more noble destiny than we were living out. We resonated to his words as he set forth his prophetic vision.

I say to you today, my friends, that in spite of the difficulties and frustrations of the moment I still have a dream.

I have a dream that one day this nation will rise up and live out the true meaning of its creed: "We hold these truths to be self-evident; that all men are created equal."

I have a dream that one day on the red hills of Georgia the sons of former slaves and the sons of former slaveowners will be able to sit down together at the table of brotherhood.

I have a dream that one day even the state of Mississippi, a desert state sweltering with the heat of injustice and oppression, will be transformed into an oasis of freedom and justice.

I have a dream that my four little children will one day live in a nation where they will not be judged by the color of their skin but by the content of their character.

I have a dream today.

I have a dream that one day the state of Alabama, whose governor's lips are presently dripping with words of interposition and nullification, will be transformed into a situation where little black boys and black girls will be able to join hands with little white boys and white girls and walk together as sisters and brothers.

I have a dream today.

I have a dream that one day every valley shall be exalted, every hill and mountain shall be made low, the rough places will be made plain, and the crooked places will be made straight, and the glory of the Lord shall be revealed, and all flesh shall see it together.

Another commonly mentioned name was Mahatma Gandhi. Fresh from seeing the motion picture about his life, these young people were stirred by the ways in which this man, living out the Sermon on the Mount, had profoundly altered the course of history for India and Britain.

I had to agree that Gandhi's heroic call to nonviolent opposition to tyranny, his compassionate plea for people to recognize their common sacred humanity, and his hope for a world in which spiritual sensitivity to all living creatures might prevail all amounted to a message for our time.

As our discussion continued there was one, above all others, who all of these bright and idealistic young people agreed had the traits of a prophet and the message we most need to hear. This was St Francis of Assisi.

St Francis of Assisi

The suggestion that St Francis could be a prophet for our
time took me by surprise. It seemed strange that a medieval
saint of the Roman Catholic Church should be the voice that
a group of Protestant young people thought would be most
relevant to our time. But these young people knew more
about St Francis than I had imagined, and their case for him
being the saint for our times proved increasingly convincing.
There is something intriguingly attractive about the pre-
Renaissance man who called himself "a clown for God".
There is a mystical quality about his character that has a
magnetizing effect on people like us.

St Francis for Today

I am sure if St Francis were with us today, he would not so
much condemn us for our consumer-oriented materialism as
he would weep over our failure to see where life and love can
be most fully experienced and actualized – among the poor.
He would not so much tell us that having things is bad as
he would tell us that giving what we have to the poor can
enliven us to God and to the highest potentialities of our
humanity.

For Francis, being Christian was, above all else, being
committed to and in love with the poor. Like many of the
modern Liberation Theologians, Francis found in the poor
a special presence of God, and he made loving the poor
synonymous with loving Christ. He said: I love the poor,
not because they are poor but because Jesus is in them.
Whenever I embrace them I embrace Our Lord.

To Francis, the poor were sacramental. He found infused
in their personhood the real presence of Christ. He was
convinced that as he embraced the poor he embraced the Lord
Himself. Jesus is there not only symbolically; according to

Francis, He is *really* there. It made no difference to him whether the poor were holy or Christian. Even among the most despicable of them, Francis contended that he could experience Christ's real presence. To him, Matthew 25:40 was to be taken literally.

Undoubtedly, the dispostion of Francis to the poor was grounded in his own personal experience. According to his own report, his understanding of who is in the poor was revealed to him through a dramatic event in his own life.

While Francis was travelling by horseback down a lonely road, a begging leper dressed in rags suddenly blocked his way. Lepers had always been a repulsive sight to Francis. He became nauseated just being near them. And there before him was a leper who could not be avoided.

At that moment Francis heard the words of Jesus resounding in his heart: "As you do it to the least of these, my brothers, you do it to me!"

Francis climbed off his horse and went up to the leper. He not only gave him all of his money but also gave him his clothes. Then, on impulse, he embraced the leper and kissed him.

Climbing back onto his horse, Francis glanced down toward where the leper had been to bid him farewell. Shocked, he realized that the road was empty. The leper had vanished. All that Francis could conclude was that he whom he thought had been a leper had really been the Lord Himself. What he had done for that leper, Francis was convinced, he had done for Christ.

In the light of that experience, it is easy to understand why Francis would consider every poor person a kind of incarnation of the resurrected Lord, waiting to be loved and served. It is also easy to understand why Mother Teresa, a twentieth-century counterpart of St Francis, should say that whenever she looks into the eyes of the poor she literally sees

Jesus looking back at her. Nor is it any wonder that this group of young Christians should find in Francis the model for their lives and a prophet for our times.

We do not need some wild-eyed pulpiteer condemning us for our consumer-oriented ways as much as we need such a wet-eyed saint, pleading with us to find fulfilment and ecstasy in service to the poor. We need this kind of pleading voice urging us to find the Eternal in the faces of the oppressed.

The Franciscan Commitment to Peace

St Francis also was comitted to peace, which makes him attractive to my young friends. Their generation has become cynical about wars, and they are not about to be hoodwinked by the slogans of politicians. They know that economic interests lie behind the propaganda about saving people from totalitarianism. Whether it be in El Salvador or in the Middle East, the real reason for Western intervention is to hold on to the resources that keep our consumer-oriented society going. And these young people have had enough. They long for a voice that will put the sacredness of human life above the values of the affluent way of life. They find that voice in St Francis.

With Francis, peace was not just an absence of war created by a balance of power. Instead, it was an attitude toward those who would define themselves as enemies. Francis would have no part of the Crusades, which in his day were obligatory service for those who would be devout Christians. He could not look on the Muslims as persons to be hated and slain any more than he could look that way on his Lord. He had only one goal as far as the followers of Islam were concerned, and that was to tell them about Jesus and help them to realize that in Jesus they could all be brothers and sisters.

With some of the members of his order Francis went out

one day to meet those so-called enemies of the cross. He did not go with a sword or a bow; he went armed only with love and grace. He must have seemed like a crazy man to those worshippers of Allah who knew how to do only one thing to the Christians who challenged them. Yet there must have been a mystical presence about that son-of-merchant-turned-saint. There must have been something awesome about that strange man dressed in hessian with a piece of rough rope tied around his waist.

Surprisingly, the enemy army received him as an honoured guest and gave him an audience with their sultan. Nobody knows what Francis said and did in the sultan's tent. It may have been that Francis talked theology and did a bit of Christian apologetics. But I think not. I have a sense that this simple monk did nothing more and nothing less than love the sultan and share with him the source of that love, who is Christ Jesus.

There is no indication that the sultan was converted, and there is every indication that Francis was disappointed. He would be neither the first nor the last prophet of God who would have his love rejected. But he tried. And to this day, he symbolizes for all of us the radical attitude toward one's enemies prescribed by Jesus. It is an attitude set forth in the Sermon on the Mount. It is an attitude seldom lived out in a world where people trust more in power than in love, and where "realism" dictates that you do in your enemy before your enemy does you in.

The early Church was pacifist, but they would turn from that pacifist posture once Constantine made Christianity the religion of the Empire. After all, the pragmatists argue, you owe a favour or two to an emperor who gives your religion such prestige. That's how the system works. And so Christendom blessed the Empire and sanctified its armies. The priests who were placed in the royal court dictated that

Constantine's wars were "holy" wars, and the cross replaced the eagle on the Roman standard.

It would be centuries before St Francis of Assisi would recover Christ's message about what to do about one's enemies. But the pacifist mindset, derived from a literal reading of the Sermon on the Mount, is gaining an ever-widening acceptance among present-day young people and among some older ones too. More and more Christians are becoming convinced that the New Testament does not allow for killing, even in battle, and they look for a prophet who will tell this to the Church.

Certainly, the Vietnam War and, more recently, the Gulf War, had a great deal to do with the pacifist inclinations these young people have, but there is a deeper reason why the Franciscan understanding of violence is increasingly taking hold of them. I think it is because it is a belief whose time has come. It is as though it is a truth that has come of age, a doctrine with an affinity for our people, a message that we, more and more, are ready to hear. What Jesus showed us about loving our enemies and how St Francis believed and practised it seems relevant and even obvious to a new breed of Christians.

When they see what is happening because of the eye-for-an-eye and tooth-for-a-tooth way of life in the ghettos, the senselessness of violence becomes more and more clear. They see the futility of killing as a way of resolving anything. And as they live and work in a culture permeated with retributive concepts of justice, they only hope to establish what Paul in 1 Corinthians 12 called "the most excellent way".

St Francis's Respect for Nature

No prophetic judgment on contemporary Western culture would be adequate without addressing the ecological disaster perpetrated because of our consumeristic ways. Our disregard for nature has resulted in the extinction of large numbers of both animal and plant species. What we have done to both the oceans and the atmosphere has raised serious doubts about the survival of life here on spaceship earth. In such a context, it is easy to see that for these young Christians what Francis taught about being related to our physical and biological environments takes on a quality of urgency.

The respect and love that Francis had for animals are legendary. While some of the tales told about this gentle monk might indeed by apocryphal, they must be at least based on truth. Whether or not he was in such empathy with nature that he was able to talk to birds is something that is impossible to prove. Nevertheless, most people are familiar with the claim and have seen pictures and statues depicting that claim. That he had a mystical relationship with animals is undoubtedly true.

There is nothing "New Age" about such claims. After all, Jesus was able to do the same. When our Lord spoke, even the winds and the waves obeyed Him. Why couldn't the man who many claim most nearly imitated Christ have done a little of the same?

According to one of the most famous stories about Francis, he was able to make a "brother" out of an animal. It seems there was a wolf who regularly attacked the herds of sheep owned by the farmers of Assisi. So many sheep were being killed that the doings of that wolf proved to be a threat to the economic wellbeing of the town. The shepherds felt that the menace posed by the wolf could no longer be ignored, and they gathered themselves together and decided to track him down collectively and destroy him. When Francis heard what the shepherds had planned, he intervened with a proposal. What he asked was for permission to go into the hills and seek out the wolf and personally deal with the creature. Only if he failed, he told them, would they then be free to hunt the wolf and kill him. The farmers agreed with Francis's plan and gave him a few days to carry it out.

When Francis returned to Assisi a few days later, the one-time terrible wolf was following along behind him like some kind of pet puppy dog. Francis had tamed the wolf with love and kindness. He had turned the beast into a friend. He had participated in a limited way with the redemption of the fallen nature.

The creatures of nature, as demonstrated by Francis, have the potential to be in sacred communion with us and even to be transformed through our love for them. We, as humans, can be like older brothers and sisters to animals. We can sense, according to Francis, a limited but, nevertheless, real kinship not only with animals but with the entire physical universe.

If we are to take Francis at his word, the stars and the planets are not to be taken as the "dead" assemblages of molecules that the physicists have told us that they are. According to Francis, we can pray for our "brother the wolf" and talk in an almost intimate way about the sun and the moon. Without hesitancy he asks of birds:

My brother birds, you ought always to praise and love your Creator who has given you feathers for clothing, wings for flight, and all that you have need of. He has given you a dwelling in the purity of the air, though you sow not, neither do you reap.

and also:

Praised be my Lord God with all his creatures and especially our brother the sun, who brings us the day and who brings us the light; fair is he and shines with a very great splendour: O Lord, he signifies to us Thee.

Praised be my Lord for our sister the moon, and for

the stars, the which he hath set clear and lovely in the heavens.

This is no sentimental pantheism (although mystics are often accused of being pantheists). Nor is it some kind of Spinozan monism (although he, like Spinoza, acknowledges some kind of spiritual solidarity with nature). It is simply part of the prayerful attitude of one who loves his Lord and is conscious that in everything that exists, God is at work keeping it together and giving it vitality.

> For by him were all things created, that are in heaven, and that are in earth, visible and invisible, whether they be thrones, or dominions, or principalities, or powers: all things were created by him and for him:
>   And he is before all things, and by him all things consist.
>   Colossians 1:16–17

Such an attitude toward nature is essential for us to learn if we are to survive in this world and have some kind of harmonious relationship with nature. We must move beyond a theology of domination of the geosphere and biosphere that allows for the exploitation of nature, and we must develop a belief system that places us in joyful empathy with nature. Of course we must avoid the kind of fuzzy anthropomorphic religiosity of animism and the kind of religio-magic occultism that mark the New Age movement. Somehow we must reestablish that respectful awe of nature that was so brilliantly modelled for us in St Francis. In some way we must learn how to revere the animals, the plants, and even the inanimate realms of nature. And we must do it without attributing more in the way of spiritual essence to nature than the Bible allows.

If we learn what St Frances can teach us, we will no longer kill the animals for sport or pollute the water and the air as we produce the things we think we need. We will no longer be aliens in a strange and distant land. Instead, we will be at home in a world ablaze with signs of holiness. We will find our rightful place in the wonder of it all.

St Francis, to my young friends, is more and more being defined as the saint for this decade. His spirituality is a model for those who would repent of the havoc wreaked on nature. We have in St Francis a glimpse of what we all should be if we are to survive into the twenty-first century.

St Francis's Familiarity with the Miraculous

There is one last thing that made St Francis the ideal prophet for these young Christians, who, in some ways, may embody the longings of a whole new Church. It was his devotional life. In his prayer life he experienced such a oneness with Christ that he, like some say was true of the apostle Paul, bore the marks of the Lord's crucifixion. Those who study the life of St Francis cannot escape the story of his wilderness experience on the mountain during which he came to bear in his body the stigmata of Christ.

An aristocrat from Tuscany named Orlando of Chiusi, upon meeting Francis, wanted to give him a gift as an act of courtesy. The gift turned out to be a strange one. It was a mountain. Not prone to accepting any gifts that would make him other than a poor man, it was surprising that Francis should accept this gift. But he did.

The mountain became a place where Francis would go for prayer and fasting. When he went there, he did not take even his closest friend, Alverno of Apennines. Thus, no one was present when "the miracle" happened. Nor is anyone sure of the date and time of the miracle. The scholars still debate such details. *What* really happened is also questionable, since Francis spoke of it to only one other person.

The most anyone knows is that while on the mountain

Francis had a vision. In it he saw in the heavens a vast winged figure that was either crucified or in the posture of a crucifixion. The vision was of colossal proportions. The whole heaven was filled with some gigantic wounded bird. The cries of pain that came from the winged revelation pierced the soul of Francis with sorrow and compassion. When the vision faded from the sky a vast silence filled the morning, and Francis came down from the mountain with the nail prints of Christ's crucifixion in his own hands.

An increasing number of Western Christians strongly identify with this kind of mysticism and with this kind of encounter with the transcendental. These people are tired of the commercialized kinds of displays of so-called miracles that are accessible by a mere flip of the TV control. They are left unsatisfied with the sterile rationalism of much theology.

When Moses came down from Sinai, his face was so radiant with the glory of God that a veil was needed to keep the children of Israel from being blinded by him. When Jacob came down from the mountain, he was so possessed by a blessing from his wrestling with "the angel of the Lord" that he was a new person. When St Francis came down from his mountain, his hands and feet bore the nail prints of His Saviour, and in his side there was a wound similar to that made by a Roman soldier who once thrust a spear into the body of the Son of Man. In Francis there was an answer to the prayer prayed by Paul:

> That I may know him, and the power of his resurrection, and the fellowship of his sufferings, being made comfortable unto his death.   Philippians 3:10

It is not the kind of experience that some more "rational" thinkers might call "religio-magic" that was of prime concern to the young people who talked with me about Francis.

Instead, it is the closeness with Christ this story points to that was the focus of their longings. They seemed tired of theologies that have all the answers and churches that "programme" them to death. These young people wanted to *experience* God. They wanted to *feel* God tingling in their hearts. They wanted some Dionysian ecstasy in the spirit. And they wanted a prophet who would condemn any church offering them less. They wanted to be alive in Christ and to have Christ alive in them. They were not asking for a sign in the sky, or a sudden rending of the natural order of things. They were asking for a prophet who would declare that there was still the possibility for the miracle that could take away the deadness of their souls.

Francis showed them how to experience that miracle. It would come in the midst of struggling and suffering in the dark. It would come in the midst of earnestly and endlessly pleading with God to explode within them. Ironically, it would come in the midst of these spiritual disciplines, but not because of them. Francis made them know that the miracle they sought comes as a *gift*. But he taught them how to "wait upon the Lord" in order to be ready for that gift. Francis made them believe that the gift could be theirs. And that is why they would make him a prophet for our times.

Chapter 3

An Ethic for Christians and Other Aliens in a Strange and Distant Land

Getting involved with the poor can convert people, and it usually does. Sometimes the conversions come while walking the streets of a Hispanic *barrio*. Sometimes they come while trying to teach educationally disadvantaged kids in some run-down council housing community. But however they come, among those who become directly and emotionally involved with people whom the world has rejected, conversions seem inevitable.

This special conversion, which belongs primarily to those who accept the challenge that the original rich young ruler refused (Mark 10:17–22), brings with it new revelations and truths. They are revelations that can tell people what a prophet might tell them if they could meet one face to face. They are revelations about their culture and about themselves that people would rather not have because they tell them of the shallowness of their discipleship and the phoniness of their spirituality. There is the discovery that is often made when people work among the poor about the failure of the Church to be the Church that Christ wanted it to be. In all of these revelations there is something that usually breaks through and forges a new state of consciousness.

This conversion at the hands of the poor makes people weep and shout angrily at their priests and preachers:

Why didn't you tell us? Why did you hide the truth from us? You knew that the real Jesus bids us come and die.

Yet you told us that if we believed right and lived decent lives we'd be okay. You knew the cost of discipleship was high. Yet you told us that all that would be required of us would be to live up to religious respectability. Why did you have us ignore the radical commandments of the Bible and why did you blind us with an easy belief that concealed the truth?

A New Breed of Christians

Throughout the West there are an increasing number who have gone through such spiritual trauma and have come out as a new breed of Christians. These new Christians are easily identifiable, although they do not as yet have a name. In the US the founders of *Sojourners* magazine once called them "post-American Christians". Some Mennonite writers refer to them as "Radical Reformation Christians". So far, no particular label has stuck. But they are out there across America, and they are growing in number.

One of the marks of this "second" conversion is a turning away from the consumeristic lifestyle of the middle classes. Those who have had it opt for a more responsible use of money. There is among them a profound repentance for having so many things they do not need when there are many who do not have what is essential to survive.

This new breed of Christian raises questions about what kind of cars they have a right to drive. They give careful consideration to the kind of clothes they have a right to buy and to the kind of places where they ought to live. These beliefs have a radical effect on their lifestyles as the following stories show.

Case Study I
In the Pacific Northwest of America, several Christian couples

have pooled their resources and talents to build their own houses. Instead of having to pay close to a million dollars in interest, as does the typical middle-class home buyer who has a long-term mortgage, they are building homes that can be had at the cost of building materials and land. With such huge savings to each young married couple there is going to be a great deal of money available to "do ministry" for people in need.

These houses are by no means ugly, squeezed-in boxes. They are designed to be beautiful. There will be colour and there will be charm. These houses will be works of art. One of the intentions of these young married couples is to show that an alternative lifestyle can be beautiful. They are out to dispel the myth that a fortune has to be spent to have what is attractive and joyful. Paintings that they themselves have created will decorate their walls and handcrafts will liven up their shelves and ledges. They are out to show that to be in the image of God who makes things beautiful requires that we make things beautiful, too. They are out to prove that the simple lifestyle need not be ugly.

Case Study II

There is a group of about two hundred people living together in a Christian community in Chicago. They call themselves the Jesus People USA. Among their many ventures are the publication of a cutting-edge magazine and the sponsoring of one of America's foremost Christian rock groups, *Rez Band*. Jesus People USA takes in all kinds of people, particularly street people who otherwise would have no home. The group has initiated a number of small businesses, including a roofing business and a cleaning business. A number of its people are into rehabilitating houses for the poor. All the money earned from these ventures is put into a common pot, and, as in the early

Church, individuals get what they require in accordance with their respective needs.

Visiting the Jesus People USA is, in some respects, a return to the counterculture lifestyles of the sixties. Their hair, their dress, and their manner give the impression that they are a baptized version of the flower people. But everyone who visits comes away with a sense that they have encountered authentic Christianity. The Jesus People USA are a wonder to behold.

Case Study III

In Pittsburgh, Pennsylvania, there are some young doctors fresh out of medical school who have modelled a sacrificial lifestyle in a profession that has been far too seduced by the allurements of big money. They have established a clinic that is housed in the basement of a church, and they are offering medical services on the basis of people's ability to pay. There are poor people who get the best kind of treatment available in today's world for little or no money.

It should be noted that there are many well-off people who go to these doctors too, but they are expected to pay what is typical for good medical care. As a matter of fact, there are many pastors in middle-class churches throughout the Pittsburgh area who encourage their people to go to this clinic, because the money paid by those who can afford to pay is what keeps the clinic going.

These young doctors could be on their way to becoming millionaires. Instead, they earn a very modest living. They have rejected the ways of the world and have become radical followers of another Great Physician. They are part of this emerging new breed of Christians who owe more of their understanding of Christianity to Dietrich Bonhoeffer than to the teachings of mainline churches. They are the fruits of a prophetic mentality that seems to be picking up momentum daily.

A Theology for the New Breed

A theology is being worked out by these radical Christians
as they carry out their grassroots efforts among the poor. It
is not some new formulation of doctrine. Actually, this new
breed of countercultural Christians is holding to what some
might call "the old-time religion". They are strikingly
evangelical and, for the most part, believe in the historical
creeds of the Church. They take the Bible as an infallible
message from God, although they remain aloof from the
debates that divide many evangelicals. When pressed, they
are likely to admit to some problems with the biblical text,
particularly with those passages that seem to prohibit women
from roles of leadership. But they seem generally unimpressed
with those erudite arguments that come from "lower" and
"higher" textual criticism. Like Mark Twain, they are not
bothered by the things about the Bible that they don't
understand; it's the things they do understand that bother
them. What Jesus says in the Sermon on the Mount and what
He says in the twenty-fifth chapter of Matthew is the focus
of their attention.

If anything makes these people unique, it is the emphasis
they put on the gospel writers. Christians, particularly
Protestant Christians, usually have learned to understand Jesus
through the eyes of the apostle Paul. Early in their spiritual
development most Protestants pick up the categories of
Pauline theology and then filter what they read in the gospels
through that grid. There is nothing wrong with this, but it
does make for an emphasis in interpreting Scripture other than
would be gained by reading the Pauline epistles from an
orientation established by first reading the gospels. If one's
basic understanding of what it means to be Christian comes
from Pauline teachings, then what is primary about being a
Christian is *believing* the right things. Thus, the doctrines

about substitutionary atonement, eternal security, predestination, and the second coming of Christ are of paramount importance.

These were the concerns I had while I was young. In the summer Bible conferences I attended, some Bible teacher usually took us through one of Paul's epistles. Bible study groups I joined always seemed to make Pauline theology the focus of attention. In fact, I cannot remember ever systematically studying the gospels during the entire time I was growing up. Once again, I must affirm that there is nothing wrong with this. It is just that it is easy when using this approach to become so preoccupied with what it is we are supposed to *believe* that we can lose sight of what we as Christians are supposed to *do*.

The gospels clarify in detail the radical nature and cost of discipleship. The gospels make us aware that obedience to Christ's commandments is at the core of what it means to love Christ and to be part of His Kingdom. If you think about it, you will realize that it really *does* make a difference if you read the gospels through the perspective provided by the epistles or if you read the epistles through the perspective provided by the gospels. The difference is not a matter of truth but a matter of emphasis. The epistles emphasize doctrine and the gospels emphasize lifestyle.

This new breed of radical Christians tends to take the gospels quite literally. These people make obedience to the lifestyle prescribed by Christ their primary objective. While believing in all the Pauline doctrines that are so dear to those of us who claim to hold to orthodox theologies, their primary concerns seem to be focused on how, out of gratitude to God for His grace, they can be faithful imitators of His Son.

Recognizing this emphasis on the lifestyle prescribed by Christ, it is not surprising that these radical counterculture Christians should derive much of their inspiration from the heroes and the heroines of Roman Catholicism. They are more prone to read what Thomas à Kempis wrote than what Calvin wrote. They are more likely to be awed by Mother Teresa than by famous Protestant preachers. And they are more inclined to believe that St Francis got to the heart of what the Gospel is about than they are inclined to be impressed with the writings of Martin Luther.

Some Warnings to These "New" Christians

While there is much to admire in the new counterculture Christians who seem to be popping up everywhere, there is also something a bit frightening about them. They often give the rest of us a sense that they have espoused a new legalism. Those in the old Fundamentalist subculture made giving up dancing, movies, and booze the evidence of being *really* born again. Now these new "simple lifestyle" Christians tend to come across as suggesting that only those who are radically committed to being anti-establishment have any hope of being part of the Kingdom of God.

Both to the earlier Fundamentalists and to those who promote a radical commitment to the literal message laid down in the Sermon on the Mount there comes the declaration that we are saved by *grace* and not by *works* (Ephesians 2:8–9). That means Jesus did what was necessary to make us acceptable to God and that we do not have to do a lot of good things to earn His favour. While radically embracing a Franciscan way of life at the tail end of the twentieth century may be a good form of rebellion against the spiritually stifling effects of a consumer-oriented society, it does not make us into people worthy of going to heaven. While giving up the things our culture has conditioned us to crave and experiencing God's presence in ministry to the poor may be the most "reasonable service" (Romans 12:1) to offer to Him, such things do not determine His love for us. The good news is that He loves us anyway and nothing can change that.

A moving expression of grace was provided by the parents of a graduate of the college where I teach when their son, a young Korean man, was brutally and senselessly murdered on the streets of Philadelphia. In Ho Ho had graduated with honours from Eastern College and was in the process of completing graduate studies in medicine at the University of Pennsylvania when he was killed. While mailing a letter to his family in Korea, he was surrounded by a gang of teenage thugs, robbed of the change in his pockets, and beaten to death.

Even though there are murders daily in the City of Brotherly Love, the ugliness and callous nature of this murder sent shock waves through the city. The police went all out to find the culprits and within three days had them behind bars.

The murderers proved to be a sorry lot. They were homeless boys who had grown up on the streets, "throw-away" kids unwanted by anyone. They were illiterate and unskilled and had learned to survive in their cold and violent ghetto by becoming cold and violent themselves.

When the trial of these murderers was held, In Ho Ho's parents flew to America to be in attendance. They sat motionless all during the legal proceedings. They said nothing at all during the trial. They only asked for an opportunity to speak after the "guilty" verdict was announced. It was then that they stepped forward and kneeled in front of the judge's bench.

Before a stunned audience, these parents begged for mercy for their son's murderers. Not only were they devoid of any "eye for an eye and tooth for a tooth" mentality, but they wanted to help these despicable young men.

They begged the judge to release their son's murderers to

them so that they could give the boys the home and care they had never had. They were Christians, they explained to the judge, and they wanted to show something of the grace they had received from God to those who had done them such grievous evil.

The judge, who newspaper reporters claimed had a reputation for being hard and unemotional, had tears in his eyes as he explained, "That is not the way our system of justice works."

Indeed, it is not!

The good news about the grace of God is that it isn't earned by goodness and it is handed out to those who are completely undeserving. That, of course, is why I am sure it applies to me. No intense commitment to literally living out the Sermon on the Mount and no embracing of a Christian counter-cultural lifestyle can earn God's love. It is a free gift waiting to be accepted.

A Recognition of Mid-Range Christians

Another thing that worries me about those whose embracing of the prophetic message leads them to break completely with the ways of our consumer-oriented society is their lack of patience with any of us who do not go "all the way" with them. Too often I have felt like a third-class Christian around these people because I have a house in suburbia and drive a half-decent car. Those who live in grander style, have "establishment-type" jobs, and on occasion go to faraway and exotic places for their holidays sometimes are made to feel that they have no right to claim to be followers of Jesus. What the countercultural Christians fail to realize is that there are a lot of us who have sensed the call of the prophetic message and are aware of the spiritual bankruptcy of our culture who may not be ready or able to abandon completely a lot of the things that go with the "good life". They do not seem to realize that in addition to those who drop everything to follow Jesus, there are some of us who do not go the whole nine yards, but who still make *some* changes and do *some* things that are signs of the Kingdom.

There are some of us who are what I will call *mid-range Christians*. We believe in the message of the prophet but are still a part of "the system". We relate to those who call us to a simple lifestyle, but we still have a family to raise and we want to raise them well and send them to university. We still have bills to pay. We may even be married to people who don't understand our vision. We know all of those biblical admonitions about going halfway and being lukewarm, and we confess an uneasiness about them. But we still contend that *something is better than nothing*. We still believe there is something we can do to change our world and culture even if we fall far short of the likes of Mother Teresa. We will not throw up our hands and give up, just because we cannot do all that we know we are supposed to do if we are to be a Kingdom people.

We believe that we mid-range Christians can carry out mid-range projects that will do a lot of good. What we give after office hours may not seem like much to the radically committed, but we believe that we make a difference. While we still spend a lot of money for things we don't need, we nevertheless find some joy in sending a monthly gift to support a Third-World child with Tear Fund or World Vision or in supporting a hospice for people with AIDS. So give us a break!

In the days of the early Church there were many who sold all they had and made their resources available for the work of God. Barnabas may have been the best of them. Special note is made of him in the fourth chapter of Acts.

There must have been tremendous pressure in the early Church to measure up to the standard set by Barnabas. Apparently such pressure was felt by two of those church members named Ananias and Sapphira. These two, it seems, wanting to appear as committed as Barnabas, lived a lie. They pretended to have given all, but they secretly held some of their wealth in reserve.

Peter's response to the action of Ananias and Sapphira was severe judgment. Both were struck dead (Act 5:1–11). But Peter makes the point that it was not the holding back of money that was their sin, but the *pretence* of having given all. Concealing the truth that they were still holding on to some of their worldly possessions while grandstanding as having given all was the "lie against the Holy Spirit".

To be like Barnabas is ideal. However, many of us hold back some of what we have and cling to some of the things we have been culturally conditioned to want. We do not rationalize our possessions and lifestyle, looking for proof texts to make our case. We do not justify our actions with some convoluted theology. But we will not lie. We will tell you that we still are into our consumer-oriented lifestyle. And we will also tell you that we are making strides toward change. We are not what we should be, but we are not what we were.

If you are one of us, take hope. We are doing something to break the hold on our consciousness that the world once held. It is hard going. The limited things we accomplish mean *something* in the grand scheme of things. Remember, we are saved by a King who promises that even a glass of water given in his name will have its reward (Matthew 10:42). We are the mid-range Christians. We are not as courageous as some of our brothers and sisters who have taken a great leap of faith perhaps, but we are definitely on the move, and are willing to be changed. Have patience with us, the Lord hasn't finished with us yet.

Chapter 4

The "Bottoms Up" Revolution

Some years ago, I took a group of my students from Eastern College on a study tour of the Dominican Republic. While there, we visited a *barrio* in the capital city, Santo Domingo. I wanted my students to experience firsthand the influence of the charismatic movement that had been sweeping across Latin America.

I had come to know a Roman Catholic priest in this particular *barrio* whose ministry had been dramatically transformed as the result of a Pentecostal experience. This priest was into speaking in tongues and carrying out faith healings. His Sunday morning congregation had grown from a mere handful to several hundred worshippers.

There were reports of spiritual revival throughout this slum area. There were large numbers of personal conversions and changed family life. The people who had opened themselves up to this new kind of spirituality were dramatically altering their lifestyles. Prostitutes were giving up "the game" and settling down to being respectable mothers. Men were marrying the women who had borne their children and were becoming responsible fathers. A school had been started. A clinic had been established. A literacy programme had been put into place.

I wanted my students to take a look at this Pentecostal revival in process and to explore how personal conversions work themselves out in social change. I had planned for them to begin their encounter with this priest and his ministries. I wanted them to experience the spiritual dynamism that could be generated by a simple Sunday morning Mass. None of us was prepared for what we were about to see and hear.

We arrived at the church about half an hour before the service was supposed to start. The breeze-block building with its tin roof was already filled, and we were glad to find some standing room at the back. During the half hour that followed at least a couple of hundred people showed up too late to get in and had to stand outside and listen to the service via a public address system.

The tropical temperature was already more than we were used to, and the body heat generated by the press of bodies in these squeezed quarters made conditions almost unbearable. What was immediately noticeable was that there did not seem to be any of the jovial spirit that I had come to expect from such Pentecostal gatherings. Instead, there was a sense of solemn concern among the people. There was an air of serious anticipation as the congregation waited for the service to begin.

My students and I were soon to learn that the people of this *barrio* were facing a painful future. In order to develop the tourist trade, the government had decided to tear down their *barrio*. It was located on the bank of the only river that flowed through the city, and government officials had decided that it was the ideal place to construct a marina to serve the tourist trade. The idea that these people, who were squatters with no legal rights to the land on which their shacks had been built, were to be displaced in order to create a playground for rich people with yachts, came across to us as the worst kind of economic oppression.

Each week the priest, along with a group of representatives from the *barrio*, would go to the government offices and plead for some relief from the impending disaster. Then on Sundays, during Mass, the priest would report on how the negotiations had gone. The people listened in rapt attention as the priest told them what had happened during the discussions at the presidential palace. The intensity of the listening gave obvious evidence of the urgency of the situation. The discussions were about these people's survival.

When the priest had finished his report, he allowed for questions from the congregation. One young man seated in the front row of the church rose and asked, "But, Father, what if all of these talks fail? What if all you try to do comes to nothing and they come with bulldozers to destroy our homes? What will we do then, Father? What will we do then?"

But before the priest could answer, another voice took control of the crowd. A young man standing close to us at the rear of that overcrowded church shouted out, "Then I will fight them! If they come to destroy our homes, I will fight them!"

Then, in a move that had overtones of demagoguery, he shouted at the crowd, "Are you with me? Are you with me?"

Without hesitation, the people shouted back at him, "We are with you! We are with you! We are with you!" The applause and cheering that followed was deafening.

In the midst of this turmoil the priest screamed out, "Silence! Silence!" And as the crowd fell still, he reached for the eucharist, held up the cup and declared, "In this coming struggle, Jesus is with you, too!"

Welcome to Liberation Theology

Later in the afternoon, my students got together with me. Visibly shaken by what had transpired at the morning Mass, they wanted to talk about what it all meant. Convinced that a violent confrontation was inevitable, it seemed to them that there were only three ways of looking at the situation:

1. Jesus is not involved in such political situations. If this is the case, then He is irrelevant to what is really important in the lives of these people.

2. Jesus sides with government authorities in spite of their oppression of the poor. In which case, God legitimates tyranny.

3. Jesus sides with the poor and the powerless in their struggle against the established order and joins them in their opposition to oppression.

The idea that God might side with the poor and oppressed in their efforts to resist injustice was a whole new way of thinking for my students. The idea that God might side with Marxist revolutionaries against the ruling establishment was hard for them to accept. Going along with Romans 13:13, they had always believed that those who ruled were ordained by God to do so. However, given the options available to these poor people, they changed their minds and most of them agreed that a righteous God would have to stand with the poor in their struggle for justice. "Welcome to Liberation Theology," I said to them.

That, for the sake of justice, God sides with the poor and oppressed against the rich and the powerful is not a perspective owned solely by Liberation Theologians. Indeed, any careful reading of the Bible itself might lead many others to this same conclusion. In the history of Israel, the Scriptures tell how, when the Jews found themselves enslaved in Egypt, Yahweh spoke to them and told them that He had heard their cries. The God of the Jews declared Himself to be a God who would fight for them and deliver them from their oppressors and would lead them into the Promised Land.

Later in Israel's history, when the Jews had become established in a land of their own, their God again revealed Himself to be a God who champions the cause of the poor and the oppressed. In the class struggle that took place within the life of Israel, Yahweh again and again showed that He stands with the downtrodden and the weak. Whenever the rich and the powerful made life hard for the poor and oppressed, Yahweh would send His prophets to rail against the perpetrators of suffering. Whether it was from Isaiah, Jeremiah, Amos, or Micah, the cry was always the same: God expected justice from His people more than anything else. The prophetic message from God is clear:

> He hath shewed thee, O man, what is good; and what doth the LORD require of thee, but to do justly, and to love mercy, and to walk humbly with thy God?
>
> Micah 6:8

The New Testament picks up the same theme. The birth of Jesus was heralded by the Virgin Mary, declaring to the world that her Son would be the deliverer for the socially disinherited and would bring hope for those who had no hope:

> And Mary said, My soul doth magnify the LORD,
>   And my spirit hath rejoiced in God my Saviour.
>   For he hath regarded the low estate of his handmaiden: for, behold, from henceforth all generations shall call me blessed.
>   For he that is mighty hath done to me great things; and holy is his name.
>   And his mercy is on them that fear him from generation to generation.

He hath shewed strength with his arm; he hath scattered the proud in the imagination of their hearts.

He hath put down the mighty from their seats, and exalted them of low degree.

He hath filled the hungry with good things; and the rich he hath sent empty away.

He hath helped his servant Israel, in remembrance of his mercy;

As he spake to our fathers, to Abraham, and to his seed forever.   Luke 1:46–55

The followers of Jesus preached and wrote the same message. Certainly the book of James makes it clear that Yahweh is a God who cannot tolerate the exploitation of the poor and the oppression of the defenceless by those with power and wealth.

Go to now, ye rich men, weep and howl for your miseries that shall come upon you.

Your riches are corrupted, and your garments are motheaten.

Your gold and silver is cankered; and the rust of them shall be a witness against you, and shall eat your flesh as it were fire. Ye have heaped treasure together for the last days.

Behold, the hire of the labourers who have reaped down your fields, which is of you kept back by fraud, crieth: and the cries of them which have reaped are entered into the ears of the LORD of Sabaoth.   James 5:1–4

There are as many as six hundred passages of Scripture that makes us aware that God has a special commitment to the poor. This is because He is a God who loves justice, and it is the poor who are usually the victims of injustice.

We mid-range Christians buy into this view of God. And while we are not about to take up arms against the ruling establishment, we nevertheless work for justice for the oppressed and help the poor. We are part of what futurologist Tom Sine calls "The Mustard Seed Conspiracy". By establishing within our society a variety of programmes and projects that express a love and concern for the poor that runs counter to the values of our consumer-oriented society, we believe we can gradually permeate that society with a new ethos. We believe that we can, through our mid-range projects, be what the Bible calls "leaven".

There is a belief among us that the feelings and the thinking of the West can be changed this way. We believe ours is also a kind of Liberation Theology, but it is one of positive nonviolent activism that affirms God is at work in our societies and cultures, transforming them from the bottom up. And we believe that those who participate with God in what He is doing through our mid-range "Mustard Seed" projects will themselves be transformed in the process.

Christians in the nineties want to become personally involved in meeting the needs of suffering people. Their opting for mid-range projects stems from a desire to have hands-on experiences and a longing to see direct results from their efforts. They have begun to discover what happens to them emotionally when they are doing things that make a difference in the lives of people whom they know personally.

Youth leaders are finding that the teenagers in their youth groups experience great spiritual renewal and significant consciousness raising by doing such things as running a soup kitchen for down and outs or projects to raise money for the Third World such as the Christmas Cracker and Radio Cracker programmes of recent years.

Pastors are discovering that the laity comes alive to the relevance of the Gospel when they are personally involved in ministries to the poor and oppressed. Those who are directly involved in tutoring the educationally disadvantaged, working with ghetto delinquents, creating jobs for the unemployed, and caring for the homeless turn out to be the most spiritually zealous of all church members. Praxis, the transformation of personality through involvement in direct social action, is becoming a primary means of converting people into a deeper understanding of the Christian faith.

One powerful example of this can be found in a former president of the USA.

Habitat for Humanity

A brilliant example of the shift to middle-range programmes for social change can be found in the most recent work of former president Jimmy Carter. Since leaving office, Carter has continued to be active in working for social change on the macro level. He has been negotiating with some of the key leaders of Africa to end wars and to facilitate nation building. He is still a major player in the affairs of the Middle East. His continuous influence in world affairs is such that *Time* magazine now considers him one of the best ex-Presidents we have ever had. Yet, for all of his accomplishments in negotiating social justice and peace in recent years, he has gained his greatest recognition for his work with a Christian missionary organization known as Habitat for Humanity.

Habitat for Humanity is a movement started by a Georgian neighbour to Carter named Millard Fuller. Committed to building houses for poor people who could otherwise never hope to own homes of their own, Fuller organized this movement that now is doing work in over 450 communities across the United States and around the world.

Each day as many as six houses are completed and offered to poor families at only the cost of construction. No down payment is required, and the long-term mortgages provided involve no interest payments. Fuller established this no-interest principle after reading Scriptures. He applied the Mosaic doctrine that when money is lent to the poor, it should be done without interest.

> If thou lend money to any of my people that is poor by thee, thou shalt not be to him as an usurer, neither shalt thou lay upon him usury.   Exodus 22:25

It was permissible, according to his reading of the Bible, to charge the rich interest, because when the rich borrow money it is usually to invest and to make more money. Therefore, it seems only fair to charge interest to the rich so that the lenders can share in the profit. But when the poor borrow money it is usually because they are desperate, and the Bible requires that they not be exploited by those who have the means to help them. This principle became basic to the Habitat for Humanity philosophy.

The price of these housing units is incredibly low. This is primarily because the poor families that buy them are charged only what it costs to build them. Building materials are often donated and volunteers do the construction work. Consequently, poor families can buy homes for themselves with monthly payments that are dramatically less than what they would have to pay if they were renting.

Among those volunteers who drive nails, saw wood, and hang tiles is the former president of the United States. In Philadelphia, New York, Charlotte, Atlanta, and a number of other cities across America, Jimmy Carter's involvement with the work of Habitat for Humanity has brought this organization extensive press coverage and high visibility. It has also enabled Carter to do on the grassroots level what he tried to do as President on the macro level.

In 1975, when Carter initiated his drive for the White House, he chose to do so with a speech he delivered in a burned-out section of the Bronx district of New York. Standing on a pile of rubble located on Charlotte Street, he declared that he would make the rebuilding of America's cities a primary goal of his administration.

It did not happen as Carter had hoped. When he left the presidency in 1980, the cities of America were more deteriorated than ever. His macro plan for urban renewal had failed. The attempt to provide decent housing through a government agency did not work as it should have.

Today, Carter is still addressing the same problem – the elimination of substandard housing among the poor. But now he is doing it on the local level. Working though Habitat for Humanity chapters in cities and towns all across America, he is seeing thousands of new homes being built. Working alongside small groups of Christian people, he is bringing about change. He is part of a grassroots reformist movement that is full of hope.

Carter would be the last to say that this effort on the micro level is all that is needed. Despite this, he, like so many other activist Christians, is doing what can be done through direct efforts for people in need.

Prison Fellowship – Fallout from Watergate

Another remarkable example of a person who was involved in ordering society on the macro level and is now focused on grassroots programmes is found in Charles Colson. The name is familiar to any who followed the unfolding of the Watergate scandals during the presidency of Richard M. Nixon in the early 1970s. Colson was chief counsel for the

White House during the Nixon years, and, in that position, played a key role in the Watergate cover-up. He was tried, and found guilty, and sent to prison.

Something happened to Colson on his way to jail. He became a Christian. Concerned men who live in the Washington area and who call themselves The Fellowship reached out to him during this time of adversity and shared with him their understanding of the Gospel. Having nowhere else to turn for help, Colson turned to Christ and found in Him hope and salvation. Colson had what is commonly referred to as a "born-again" experience. His life was radically changed, and he committed himself to Christian service.

It did not take Colson long to discover a mission that would occupy him for years to come. While in prison, he discovered an unmet need. He encountered men and women who had been ignored by the Church, pushed around by society, and often forsaken by family and friends. He met fellow prisoners who had failed to get due process from the law. He even found men who did not know why they were in jail. Prison became a place of revelation and calling. He made a decision to do something about all of this, and upon release he founded Prison Fellowship.

The programme of Prison Fellowship is relatively simple. It involves getting ordinary Christians to do what they can to express loving concern for those behind bars in their local communities. Within a few years of its inception, laypeople around the world were organizing into local chapters of Prison Fellowship. The ministries of these chapters consist of evangelism, personal counselling, and providing whatever help is possible to those in jail. Through evangelistic programmes and personal discussions with prisoners, thousands have been led to make commitments to Christ. In cooperation with local churches, arrangements have been worked out to provide the kind of supervised personal care necessary for those released from prison. Church people find them jobs and places to live. Support groups are made available to love and encourage these ex-convicts. Working through local churches, Prison Fellowship has been able to set up a system that minimizes the recidivism among former convicts and helps them to re-enter society successfully. All of this is done at the grassroots level.

Prison Fellowship also works for prison reforms. But its efforts to make prison treatment more humane are carried out primarily by Christians working in their own communities. Usually it is through direct discussion with the wardens that those in Prison Fellowship work to bring about changes. While those in Colson's organizations are also diligent in trying to implement progressive reforms in penal policy on both regional and national levels, they seek change primarily through their local chapters.

A few years ago, I attended a national conference for those doing prison work. I listened attentively and sadly as psychologists, criminologists, law enforcement officers, and members of the judicial system gave reports and expressed opinions. The conference was depressing, to say the least. Speaker after speaker spoke of the hopelessness of their efforts. They told of the near inevitability that those released from prison would repeat their crimes. They explained how prisons, rather than being correctional institutions, were, in reality, schools for crime. I heard how those who go to jail get labelled and moulded into criminals and, upon ending their incarceration, live out what they have learned. The reports were defeatist, and those at the conference seemed to exhibit resignation to what the penal system and those who were in it had become.

The one bright spot on the programme was the presentation made by those involved with Prison Fellowship. Their spokespeople gave reports of people whose lives had been turned around because of their encounters with Christ. There were even a couple of ex-cons on hand to give testimonies of how Prison Fellowship had led them to salvation. The only thing that surprised me was that all of those present did not immediately sign up with Prison Fellowship. It seemed to me to have the only programme that was working.

The Value of the Person in the Workplace

In the United States, locally based social change is also evident in the work of Wayne Alderson and his "Value of the Person" movement. In what is probably one of the best-kept secrets in contemporary Christendom, Alderson has come up with a way to bring the Gospel to bear in labour-management relations. Through his efforts, a significant change has taken place in what goes on between union leaders and management in companies as large as the 3M Corporation, with its thousands of employees, and others such as Shaped Wire, with its fifty employees.

The way Value of the Person started explains a great deal about why it exists. For three years, from 1972 to 1974, Alderson was the vice-president of operations at Pittron Steel in Pittsburgh. When he took over that position, the company was on the verge of bankruptcy with a future that offered little hope for a turnaround. A primary reason for the sad condition of the company was the strained relationships between labour and management. The hostilities generated by strikes and the threat of strikes had taken their toll on the company. Low morale was reflected in poor-quality work. Mutual distrust had crippled Pittron's capacity for production.

The biggest problem, in Alderson's eyes, was the humiliation that the workers of the company had been forced to endure at the hands of the former management team. As far as Alderson was concerned, the employees of Pittron simply were not valued as human beings. He decided that something had to be done to change the human dynamics of the situation. To Alderson, this was not simply a matter of good industrial management but a calling to apply his Christian faith to the affairs of the marketplace.

His efforts were directed at Sam Piccolo, the local president of the United Steel Workers. Although Alderson was a Presbyterian and Piccolo was a Roman Catholic, they soon discovered that they had a common spiritual bond. It was in the context of their shared love for Christ that Alderson made to Piccolo what must have seemed an outlandish proposal. He suggested that labour and management get together on a daily basis for prayer and Bible study.

It was a risk for Piccolo to accept Alderson's proposal. Union members generally expect their leaders to be at war with management and to treat them as the enemy. Fraternizing with management creates suspicions among the rank-and-file members and fosters the fear that the leadership has sold them out. Union leaders who are friends with those in management are usually accused of making what are referred to as "sweetheart deals" that result in settling for less than the workers feel they deserve. Nevertheless, the risk was taken and the two men invited anybody who wanted to come to attend a lunch-break chapel programme.

From the beginning, these overtly Christian gatherings drew a significant proportion of the work force. Some came out of curiosity. Others came out of suspicion. But a good number came out of deep spiritual need.

Many were tired of the animosities that had haunted their plant. Some had deep personal problems that warranted prayer. Still others came because they longed for the dignity that the sons and daughters of God gain in the context of worship. Most of them were not churchgoers. Few of them considered themselves religious. All of them felt awkward. But they came.

Over the weeks and months that followed, a remarkable change occurred at Pittron. Labour and management still had their differences. Problems still needed to be solved. Anger was still something the Pittron family had to deal with. But trust had begun to grow between these hitherto combatants. An appreciation was developing between those on each side. And, most surprising, the company had begun to turn around. Production was up. Quality control was showing a remarkable improvement. Surprisingly, this almost defunct company was beginning to show a profit.

Unfortunately, this is not one of those "and they lived happily ever after" stories. The profitability of the company made it the target of a takeover, and when Pittron fell into new hands, the new owners brought with them their own management team. Alderson found himself out of a job.

Calvinists who look for the sovereign hand of God in all that happens would have no difficulty explaining this turn of events. Alderson's departure from Pittron freed him to travel around the country telling the story of "The Miracle of Pittron".

It was not long before Alderson got together with another union leader, Lefty Scumaci, and initiated the Value of the Person seminars. Packaging what they had learned from their Pittron experiences, these two men began running seminars for companies across America. Boldly Christian, these seminars bring hitherto warring parties together, help them to confront each other honestly and in love, and encourage the correction of bad situations.

Based on these seminars, remarkable changes have been introduced into the workplace. In the words of one enthusiastic union man, "They are treating me like a person now. They used to treat me like a machine." Management leaders and union workers are learning to implement biblical principles in their relationships with one another. "Love, Dignity, and Respect" is the motto of the Alderson/Scumaci team, and in the more than one thousand companies to which this team has carried the Value of the Person message, testimonies abound as to how these values have influenced the workplace.

I can personally attest to the validity of the effectiveness of these Value of the Person seminars. I have been a part of them and have witnessed the group dynamics that occur. I have seen tough-looking union leaders break down and cry as they relate the feeling of alienation and humiliation they have experienced at the hands of management. I have witnessed managers asking union members for forgiveness and offering hope for reconciliation. I have listened as managers have talked about the betrayal and cheating they have had to endure at the hands of union workers, and I have watched union leaders repent and ask for forgiveness.

The Value of the Person seminars have a low profile in the United States. There is no fanfare in the national press to herald what is being accomplished through them. No television specials describe what Alderson and Scumaci are doing. Nevertheless, working on the local level, they may have done more to facilitate reconciliation between labour and management than all the arbitration boards and schemes sponsored by the government put together. Undoubtedly, scores of strikes have been prevented and a whole new style of management has been introduced because of the quiet "leavening" influence being exercised by these seminars.

Tom Kelly – Local Hero

Tom Kelly is an unobtrusive man. If you met him in the street you'd probably walk right past him. Yet in his hometown of Derry, in the northwest corner of Northern Ireland, he's the invisible local hero. For Tom is the city's community artist, and has been painting it red – and grey and green and yellow and blue – on street gables, underground walkways, on pub walls, indeed, anywhere the community wants and asks him to.

As Tom explains: "Most murals in Northern Ireland are of a political nature, for one side or another, so they're only up for three or four weeks before they're defaced. This one," he points at a nearby gable wall decorated by a black, white and grey group portrait entitled *The Auld Days*, "Is up for over three years and is still intact. That says something."

Tom, a Christian from Derry's Catholic Bogside area, is a community artist, and sees his job and faith as quietly helping build bridges between the Catholic and Protestant communities riven by a quarter of a century of violence and murder. The Auld Days, set in the 1950s, typifies his approach – get the local community involved in selecting a photograph of the area pre-Troubles, then have the young people from the same area help paint it.

And the location is important too. As Tom explains: "When the Troubles started this was a very important area insofar as just about all the petrol bombs in the Battle of the Bogside were made on this site, 22 years ago. It's deliberately done in black and white because it reflect in an indirect way the attitudes of the isolation in Northern Ireland – but there's quite a bit of grey there too, which is where I probably fit in."

Tom Kelly sees his work as having a two-fold purpose. "It reminds the old people of what sort of a community they once had – healthy in one sense, pretty bad in another. But the community spirit was there, and it also reminds the young of where their parents were born and how they lived at that time. The murals help give them a sense of heritage and of the past as well."

He is equally comfortable working in both Republican and Loyalist areas, a policy he is keen to emphasize, given the avowedly non-sectarian and apolitical nature of his work. But it's the spiritual underpinning of his work that he regards as being equally important. "Art can be a universal bridge, like music," Tom says. "If my work glorifies God, whether it's in Protestant or Catholic areas is immaterial, as long as it glorifies Him and people appreciate what's being done. It's more important to be creating and building up, rather than dragging down and destroying."

Despite the continuing carnage, Tom sees hope for the future. "Some people in this city are laying down their religion – as far as being a Protestant or a Catholic is concerned – and are re-examining what Christianity is. So there are quite a few communities in Northern Ireland which are neither Protestant nor Catholic, but are simply followers of Christ in the sense that they call themselves Christian, period. That is a healthy thing.

"For me," he continues, "Christianity speaks of knowing Christians by their love for one another and by the fruit that they bear. If that fruit is violence, segregation and demonstrations, then to me it's not Christianity."

That Tom was recently asked by a Protestant area of the city to paint three huge new murals over three paramilitary ones already there testifies to the quiet influence he is having in Derry. He truly is a living embodiment of what it means to be a Christian living over society's faultlines. Tom is also an example of how one man can make a difference, how by using your God-given gifts for His glory you can help bring a spirit of reconciliation and peace into the midst of the most unsettled of situations or circumstances.

It can be done.

A Summary of Mid-Range Programmes

The mid-range approach built on the conviction that small, manageable projects in which Christians can be personally and directly involved are the most promising means for making a difference in the world.

This new style of social action emphasizes changing the world through small groups. It is a style in which Christian people in face-to-face relationships devise plans to implement God's justice where they normally live and work. It is built on the premise that when enough small victories for justice are won in the primary associations in which Christians work, play, and hold membership, these victories will have a cumulative outcome that will affect the macrostructures of society. It is a theory of social change that presupposes that the kinds of things that small independent groups can carry out will create ripple effects that gradually will flow through the entire social system.

Chapter 5

Rumblings from the Underground

If the message of the prophet is needed anywhere, it is needed on the university campuses of this nation. There are students at just about every college and university who concur with the diagnosis that apathy rules as the predominant psychic condition of the academic community. The kind of rallies and riots that marked the sixties are gone and forgotten. What was once an emotionally upset and angry student population has settled down. And while there have been a few petitions against apartheid in South Africa and some isolated forums on environmental issues, there have been few signs of the revolutionary fervour that was so evident among students during the heady days of the late sixties.

Young men and women are not "dropping out" in accord with the pleas of the old counterculture gurus. No longer do students protest and talk about changing the world for the better, as their parents dreamt a quarter-century ago. Now, again unlike their parents, for the most part, campus talk has been reduced to what money-making opportunities exist during the summer months and what job options there are after graduation.

The anti-establishment anger of the sixties seems to have been replaced by an apathetic careerism. What few protest rallies still occur seem only to mimic those of the turbulent years of the past. As far as the press and the ruling establishment are concerned, these minor upsets are to be largely ignored. If the deadness that marks our consumer-oriented society has manifested itself anywhere over the last decade or so, it has done so in the halls of academia. If indeed the prophet is a messenger from God who weeps over what has happened to God's people, then the prophet would have had much to lament upon visiting our campuses during these last few years.

But there are rumblings. In the midst of this pervading collegiate apathy, something new seems to be struggling to live. In the emotional graveyards that are all too common in the world of higher education, there appears to be something vital stirring to be born. It is not easy to discern its form or to understand its nature, but there are inklings. And those inklings are a source of hope. As the homespun American philosopher Yogi Berra once said, "It ain't over 'til it's over!" Before writing off college students, we should pay attention to these rumblings and ask if something new and dynamic is about to come out of them. Or, as the biblical prophet asked, "Will these dry bones rise again?"

These rumblings are not couched in the revolutionary rhetoric of the angry sixties. Nor do they manifest themselves in the kind of "media events" so popular with our sound-bite-conscious media culture. They have no shrill-pitched spokespersons or any clear political agenda. But they are there. Those who stop to feel their presence will find them. The rumblings are "not yet", but they are about things that are coming. The prophet of God would rejoice in them and cite them as signs of a coming Kingdom. The prophet would say they are signs of the times. The prophet would find them grounds for hope.

Signs of the Times

In London, some Christians working with the evangelical organization Oasis have set up a walk-in medical centre for down-but-not-quite-out people in the capital. The aim is to provide free medical assistance to those who really need it but have been denied access until now because they sleep rough in the streets, in doorways, concrete car-parks – anywhere they can scratch an existence, some sleep and occasional privacy, but certainly not what could be called a living, as they forage through the dustbins and castoffs of others.

Elsewhere in the city, in the crypt of St Botolph's Church, Aldgate, near the capital's financial heart, up to 300 homeless people come together each day. With a job club, art classes, discussion groups, theatre workshops, literacy and craft classes, it helps them regain their dignity and begin to take charge of their lives again. The crypt got funding from the financial institutions nearby, as its former vicar, the Rev. Malcolm Johnson, told *The Guardian* newspaper recently. "We pointed out to the City Corporation bosses that on the streets beneath them were men and women in desperate need of help," he recalled. "That if they would provide the funds we would do the work." Which they have, with great success.

In San Diego, California, some students from a Nazarene liberal arts college organize to help people with AIDS. They refurbish a dilapidated house and get furnishings and beds. They join with a local committee composed of Christian business and professional people in opening up a hospice for the victims of this dreaded disease. The gay newspaper in the city writes them up, giving them front-page coverage. The AIDS hospice is referred to by this paper as "The House That Love Built."

In Seattle, Washington, another group of Christian students prevails over objections from some of those in their college's administration and gets part of their dormitory set aside to be a shelter for the homeless. Each evening, they get people off the streets who have no place to sleep to come and be with them in their dormitory. They feed these disinherited strangers and treat them as friends. They do not solve the problems of the homeless, but they do make a difference.

In Chicago, some students from still another Christian liberal arts college spend their weekends rehabilitating houses in the slums to provide low-cost dwellings for the poor. In the middle of an urban ghetto, they create houses of beauty that stand in stark contrast to everything around them. There, in that run-down neighbourhood, they establish signs of a coming Kingdom.

A national news network does a special on the changing behaviour of college students during spring break. Whereas in former years they all seemed to flock to such resort areas as Palm Springs, California, or Fort Lauderdale, Florida, there is a rising tendency for some of them to spend this time in community service. Working among the poor in Appalachia or on Native American reservations in Arizona, a new breed of students is demonstrating that it gets its gratification out of helping and giving.

The People of EAPE

There is a Christian altruistic spirit that is rumbling beneath the surface of our consumeristic society. In Philadelphia it expresses itself in the programme of the Evangelical Association for the Promotion of Education (EAPE), which I head. Serving people who live in the subsidized housing communities of Philadelphia and Camden, New Jersey, EAPE carries out its mission almost completely through the efforts of college-age volunteers. These young people serve full-time without pay. They come from all over the country at their own expense, live together in a large old house that was once an orphanage, and come up with their own money to pay for the food they eat. Nevertheless, they come by the hundreds.

During peak times, there are as many as two hundred of them working with up to fifteen hundred inner-city poor people on any given day. These EAPE workers run tutorial programmes for educationally disadvantaged teenagers and day camps for children who otherwise would have little to keep them occupied. Working along with the adult members of government housing communities, they foster a variety of community organizations. In conjunction with the tenants, they are initiating some small businesses in order to provide much-needed income for welfare families. A thrift shop has been established that not only creates some jobs but also makes available to the community inexpensive clothing and house furnishings. Both a lawn-care business and a pizza business have been established to create employment for teenagers. One of EAPE's most successful ventures is a greetings card business. Half a dozen former gang members have been trained by EAPE workers to print and market greetings cards and are selling enough of them to make a decent living.

Businesses like these prove to be difficult enterprises, to say the least. Teenagers who have not been raised on a work ethic and who often are school dropouts have difficulty adapting to the requisites of business. The EAPE volunteers often fail and get discouraged. Yet the efforts go on relentlessly. There is little in the way of giving up among these Christian idealists.

A number of other EAPE services are provided by these collegiate volunteers, ranging from latchkey programmes to care for children during after-school hours to job training programmes for adults. There is an endless array of clubs, Bible study groups, sports events and music groups in the EAPE ministries. And all of these activities are carried out by young people who ask for little more than an opportunity to serve others in the name of Christ. These college students volunteer in such numbers that EAPE is helping to place them in similar work settings in other cities.

There has been almost no press coverage of these self-sacrificing college students and what they are accomplishing. That is the way EAPE staff people like it. Through word of mouth, information about the opportunities to work in the EAPE programme is passed on through colleges and universities across the country.

The work force of EAPE is composed both of persons who are radically committed and those who are what I have been calling mid-range Christians. Some have given their lives to inner-city ministry among the poor and have set aside all plans for lucrative establishment-type professions. On the other hand, most of these EAPE workers have volunteered for only two years of service and are planning to go back into mainstream employment when their time is up.

EAPE is yet another example of change at the grassroots level. Its approach to social change has nothing to do with seizing power and imposing "improvements" from the top down. Instead, its young volunteers are attempting to serve on the neighbourhood level. They hope that the influences from what is accomplished there will permeate upward through the social system. They believe that macro change can start with micro projects.

Mid-Range Work in the Professions

Professional people also are picking up the prophetic message and opting to break the hold our consumer-oriented society has had on them. Some do it radically; one example is an accountant I knew who worked in a firm that would have made him rich but gave his job up to work in an orphanage in Cambodia. Like many others, he had grown tired of tiptoeing through life in order to arrive at death safely. He wanted the splendid exhilaration that belongs to those who dare to bet their lives on the cause of the Kingdom.

Most mid-range Christians adopt countercultural values only halfway and would be the first to admit that they have a long way to go to live out fully the call of Christ to forsake all. But they too have their reward.

Once, while preaching in West Virginia, I had a couple of young lawyers in the congregation. My topic that evening was the cost of discipleship. When I gave the invitation for people to commit themselves fully to Christian service, these men did not come forward. Nevertheless, they did accept the challenge to alter their lives and seek ways in which they could more fully serve Christ and the poor.

These two men practised law together, and they made a decision to offer free legal services to poor people who lived in their county. This was a decision to go way beyond the set amount of *pro bono* work (work without charge) that most law firms do. These men decided to help anyone in the county who needed their help.

Their commitment to the poor changed their lives dramatically. Not only did they become known as friends of the poor, but their good reputation brought in an avalanche of unexpected new paying customers. What was even more encouraging was that scores of people who were delinquent in the payment of fees suddenly paid up. "I suppose they didn't want to cheat lawyers who helped the poor," one of these young men explained.

They still have their BMWs, they still vacation in Bermuda, and they still have a lot of the things that "worldly" people in our consumer-oriented society make the essence of their lives. They haven't given it all up for Jesus. But they are prime examples of mid-range Christians who are doing *something* significant for Christ in their everyday lives. They are not simply slaves to the system.

If you are not going to drop everything and follow Jesus, then you, like these lawyers, ought to be asking yourself what you can be doing right where you are. Some of us, as they say, have to bloom where we are planted. For instance, if you are an accountant, look around for those charitable organizations that need somebody to audit their books. With the new levels of fiscal accountability being demanded of Christian organizations by both the government and the general public, there is probably a missionary society or a youth ministry close to where you live and work that desperately needs your help.

There is a banker I know who was all too aware of the fact that banks are reluctant to lend money to poor people. (Former US President Harry S. Truman once said that banks are institutions that lend money to people who can prove they don't need it.) This man responded to the call of Christ by setting up a savings and loan association that specializes in lending money to the poor. He has worked out a system whereby poor people are linked up with economically successful people he has recruited from churches. The latter assume responsibility to serve as consultants to the poor, showing them what goes into managing your money. For the poor who need money for things like buying a house or setting up a small business, getting the loan is contingent upon their willingness to enter into such an arrangement. The results have been most encouraging.

Poor people who were bad risks "on paper" have paid back their loans. Many people who did not know how to handle money have learned to do so. It isn't anything that makes the headlines, but what Robert Lavelle is doing is part of that Mustard Seed Conspiracy that can change our society and bring it back to life.

In rural Pennsylvania, there are a couple of car mechanics who decided to use their skills for the Kingdom of God. They have set up a small, non-profit-making organization that fixes up cars for Christian organizations. I do not know what we at EAPE would do without their help. They have made several cars and minibuses available for our use. These vehicles are absolutely essential for our work with inner-city children. And we are only one of scores of organizations that have expanded their ministries to needy people because of the commitment of these mechanics.

My friend Ron Barbaro, a top executive with the Prudential Insurance Company, had heard me speak on several occasions and knew of my concern that Christians respond with help for people who are dying of AIDS. Time and again I had painted verbal pictures in public addresses of the failure of the Church and our society to provide the compassionate care that people with AIDS need.

Ron pulled me aside one day after I had spoken and told me of a new policy that he had instituted with Prudential. He had made it possible for people who have AIDS to collect on their life insurance policies *before* they were dead. To Prudential it was no gigantic giveaway. The company would have had to pay the money sooner or later. But because of this new policy, those suffering with AIDS would be able to pay for their medical care and for other services to make their lives a little more bearable.

Ron explained to me, "I saw too many cases in which a family would abandon a guy with AIDS only to pick up his insurance cheque when he died. I thought to myself that the dying guy should have had that money. So I decided to make that kind of thing happen." This is one more example of somebody making things different by putting life and feeling into a business.

Pete and Sue Carter were my students at Eastern College. During their college years, they got involved in ministry with street kids in the Kensington district of Philadelphia. They got "hooked" on what they were doing, and when they graduated from college, they went to live in the neighbourhood where they had been working. They bought a house in a run-down community, took available jobs close by, and made being a presence for Christ in what could be called a very bad neighbourhood their primary mission in life.

It was not long before the young people who had come to know them began hanging out at their house. A few of the street kids who had no homes of their own came to live with Pete and Sue.

The effect that these two young people are having on the youth of Kensington is hard to measure. But I am convinced that they are more of the "Salt of the Earth" that Jesus has called us to be. I know that they are part of what God is doing to give new life to a dying civilization.

On the Individual Level

Perhaps one of the best examples I know of extraordinary service for the Kingdom of God being done on the micro level is the story of a young woman named Nancy. I met Nancy because she was a guest on a radio show that I host in Philadelphia. Nancy is crippled and confined to a wheelchair, yet she has developed a unique ministry to hurting and lonely people of the city. It is beautiful in its simplicity. She runs ads in the personal columns of the newspaper that read:

> If you are lonely or have a problem call me. I am in a wheelchair and seldom get out. We can share our problems with each other. Just call. I'd love to talk.

The results are astounding. Each week at least thirty calls come in. She spends her days comforting and counselling people. She has become someone to lean on for hundreds of people with problems.

When I asked Nancy how she became crippled, she answered, "By trying to commit suicide."

I was stunned. She went on to explain, "I was living alone. I had no friends. I hated my job, and I was constantly depressed. I decided to jump from the window of my apartment, but instead of being killed, I ended up in hospital paralyzed from my waist down. The second night I was in the hospital, Jesus appeared to me and told me that I'd had a healthy body and a crippled soul but from then on I would have a crippled body and a healthy soul. I gave my life to Christ right there and then.

"When I got out of the hospital, I tried to think of how a woman like me in a wheelchair could do some good and I came up with the idea of putting the ad in the newspaper. And the rest, as they say, is all history."

Following Father Abraham

In all of this talk about revolutionizing our society and culture by infusing it with new spiritual vitality and challenging our consumer-oriented lifestyle, we have not paid much attention to our so-called senior citizens. There is a tendency to assume that, after the age of fifty, people are not likely to make the bold moves or engage in the daring things that can shake the foundations of society and prepare the way for a new day and a new kind of world. But that notion is now being challenged.

What I like about the biblical story of Abraham and Sarah is that God called them to the mission of changing the world when they were old people (Hebrews 11). Abraham responded to the call when "his life was far spent", and Sarah joined in the mission "when she was past age". Imagine Abraham at ninety-four waking up one morning and shaking Sarah, his ninety-two-year-old wife, with the news, "Sarah!

Sarah! Get up! We're going to create a new humanity! A new nation! A new epoch in human history!"

The poor woman probably rolled over in her bed as she mumbled, "Go back to bed, Abe. You're confused."

"No, Sarah," he might have answered, "I had this dream. God told me! You and I are going to start a whole new race and give birth to a whole new nation!"

"How does this new race start?" Sarah must have sleepily inquired.

"Glad you asked," said Abraham, with a sly little grin on his lips. And they both fell back in bed laughing.

The next scene is Abraham and Sarah, his ninety-two-year-old wife, leaving Ur of the Chaldeans, Abraham "not knowing whither he went" as "he looked for a city which hath foundations, whose builder and maker is God" (Hebrews 11:8, 10).

"Where are you going?" their amused neighbours might have shouted out to them.

"We don't know," would have been the answer.

"Well, what do you intend doing when you get to this place you don't know about?" they might have taunted.

"We're going to build a new nation. We're going to give birth to a new people. We're going to give humanity a new beginning," the old folks would have shouted back.

Oh, that we had a host of people like Abraham and Sarah. Oh, that the millions of so-called retired people would wake up to God's calling.

With early retirement becoming more and more the norm, we are confronted with the astounding fact that 32 per cent of all men between the ages of fifty-five and sixty-four are already retired and on pensions. With all of these human resources who are financially independent and who have lifetimes of experience, you would think there would be an endless stream of volunteers for the work of the Kingdom.

You would think that the ministries to the homeless and soup kitchens would not be able to handle all the people lined up to serve. Such is not the case. Once retired, these people simply drop out. In England a lot of them go to the coast to relax and take up golf. They claim they have done their part and are now going to take it easy.

I would like to remind retired people that only once is retirement talked about in the Bible.

> And he spake a parable unto them, saying, The ground of a certain rich man brought forth plentifully: And he thought within himself, saying, What shall I do, because I have no room where to bestow my fruits: And he said, This will I do: I will pull down my barns, and build greater; and there will I bestow all my fruits and my goods. And I will say to my Soul, Soul, thou hast much goods laid up for many years; take thine ease, eat, drink, and be merry. But God said unto him, Thou fool, this night thy soul shall be required of thee: then whose shall those things be, which thou hast provided? So is he that layeth up treasure for himself, and is not rich toward God.
>
> Luke 12:16–21

The work of God needs these senior citizens if we are to break the demonic hold that consumerism has on us. The last part of life cannot be seen as merely a time to treat ourselves to all of the things society says we need in order to be happy. Life is meant to be more than travelling around in recreational vehicles towing boats. The seemingly endless days of retirement were not all meant to be spent on golf courses and in fishing boats.

Fortunately, many are rebelling against the stereotypical roles of old people. Just as in the States, no longer do they feel the need to become what journalist and social commentator Tom Wolfe once termed "the gerontoid cowboys" – people who simply retired by endlessly and pointlessly roaming around in motorized caravans since their grown-up children could not be bothered with them. No, now many retired Christians are looking on their twilight years as a new frontier and a wonderful opportunity to serve God.

Realizing this, the evangelical group CARE, Christian Action Research and Education, has launched a series of weekend seminars called CARE for the Future. These are designed to explore the challenges and opportunities of later life and promote the idea that growing older can be a positive experience and life is not just the domain of the young, as the media is so intent on insisting. And what's especially good is that it gives people opportunities to contribute a lifetime's experience to activities which benefit both the individual and the community around them.

And the Oasis Trust, too, is recognizing the potential of older Christians by encouraging them to invest a year in fulltime service in its Jubilee Project. This allows the over-50s to use and develop their skills and gifts, as well as discovering new ones, in church-based teams.

As Steve Bassett of Oasis explains: "The idea is based on the Old Testament idea of Jubilee. It was a time to thank God for his goodness by giving to others. Now the over-50s can give their own year of Jubilee back to God. We believe the older person has got much to offer."

Indeed. Among the areas the Birmingham-based Jubilee team members are involved in are pastoral visiting, leading worship, caring for new Christians, discipleship training, preaching, and schools and children's work. Just as in the United States older people such as Barb and Phil Julian, who retired from a career in the Navy, are experiencing a new lease of life by doing similar things. These two "retired" people work day and night in our programmes with youth. Having raised ten children of their own, they are well equipped to provide the stability that comes with maturity for our many young volunteers and staff workers. Recently, the Julians have been joined by a middle-aged divorced woman and a widow. These two women come from professional backgrounds and bring expertise in business and education, as well as willing spirits and loving hearts, to our ministries.

In America, Trevor's Place, a nationally known programme for the homeless, is getting an increasing number of volunteers from the retired community of Philadelphia. As a matter of fact, two of my own aunts who are in their seventies work at Trevor's Place almost daily.

President Carter's mother, Lillian, established a solid example for service by joining the Peace Corps as a senior citizen. Now thousands of older people are following her example.

These are rumblings of something new. There are inklings of a new beginning. There is hope that a group of drowsy people will wake up to their potentialities and help to awaken a nation. Those who are old must dream dreams, as Scripture says. They must realize that life was not made for consumerism or retirement. They must learn that life was made for living, and that living is serving. They must come to see that life was meant to be more than a walk between two hospitals – the one for birth and the one for death. The hour is at hand when people must come into the fullness of their humanity and rebel against the ways that society has prescribed for them to retire. They should follow instead the lead of Abraham and Sarah.

Chapter 6

The Church Is Alive and Well

Prophets have never got on well with organized religion. In ancient Israel, they picked on the priests who pretended to be the official spokesmen for God and accused them of being phonies. Jesus had less-than-harmonious relations with the priests and scribes of His day. And since His time, prophetic voices have kept up their barrage of attacks on officially ordained servants who dress in clerical garb.

The accusations seem to have a sameness to them. The religious professionals are generally condemned for being more interested in holding on to their jobs than they are in speaking the truth.

Danish philosopher Søren Kierkegaard (1813–55), who was a specialist in picking on the clergy, once said:

It is one thing to love humanity so much that you are willing to die on a cross to save humanity. It is quite another to expect to earn a big salary describing a somebody who died to save humanity.*

Of course there is always much for prophets to find wrong with the religious establishment. To gain power and wealth, the clergy have historically made peace with kings and political

*Søren Kierkegaard, *Attack upon "Christendom"*, Princeton, NJ: Princeton University Press, 1944.

leaders, giving their blessings when they should have been declaring the judgments of God. To fill their pews, preachers have too often told people what they wanted to hear instead of exposing their sinful ways. The religious establishment is commonly accused of compromising the truth in order to gain favour and praise. And church leaders, for political and economic reasons, have given "the right hand of fellowship" to people who should have been given a kick up the backside. Undoubtedly the Old Testament prophets would go hard on our comfortable churches should they speak to us today.

A young Jewish student I knew who had been converted to Christianity once expressed his disappointment with the Church by telling me, "If somebody took Jesus's teachings in the Beatitudes (Matthew 5:3–12) and decided to create a religion that contradicted those teachings, then he'd probably come up with the Protestant Church."

While that judgment is far too harsh, there is some truth to it. Whereas Jesus taught that the poor are blessed, some churches often suggest that living like a Christian is a way to financial success. Whereas Jesus taught, "Blessed are they that mourn," we seem to promise happiness and smiles. Many Church people tend to support punishment instead of mercy. And we are more known for supporting wars and rumours of wars than we are for being peacemakers. Undoubtedly, we church people too often adopt a lifestyle that is aimed at winning friends and influencing people rather than one that might lead to persecution.

There is little doubt that any real prophet who looked at the contemporary Church would criticize us most for our apparent capitulation to the value system of our consumer-oriented society. For the most part, we have remained silent in the face of the seductiveness of affluence and have had little to say about the sinful things that we as a nation do to make our way of life possible.

Prophets would rail against what we have done to the environment in order to maintain our cars and produce the things we have been conditioned to want. They would hit us hard for our willingness to support oppressive dictators in Third-World countries simply because they serve our economic interests. But most of all, they would condemn us for allowing our spiritual hungers to be replaced by the craving for things that has become the hallmark of our consumerism.

The Radical Church of the Prophets

Throughout the West, there are people who share the concerns that the prophets of God would have. These are the radical disciples who lead the way in establishing a countercultural Church that dares to declare the judgment of God upon the nation.

Perhaps the best example in America of this Church is found in the Sojourners Community in Washington, DC. Led by Jim Wallis, one of the most articulate preachers in America, this congregation has taken the lead in exposing hypocrisy in government and superficiality in Christendom. The members of the Sojourners Community have earned a reputation for being radically opposed to US policy on apartheid in South Africa, on nuclear weapons, and on the war in El Salvador. They can be counted on to be supporters of feminist issues as well as justice for gays and lesbians. They don't just talk. They march. They live dangerously.

Against our consumer-oriented society, these people have made an alternative lifestyle one of the canons of their faith. The call of Christ, as far as they are concerned, requires that we live simply so that others might simply live. Their message to the rest of us is to cut back on buying things that are not needed and to adopt measures that are ecologically responsible. Such stances, they claim, are some of the things that go with being a Christian. They are not options.

The Sojourners Community, in many ways, serves as a conscience for the rest of the churches of America. The people of this group will not let us forget that justice issues are at the core of the Gospel. Through the publication of their magazine, *Sojourners*, they keep us aware of what the US government is doing that we, as Christians, should be questioning. They represent a form of Christianity that will not be at home with the ruling political establishment but, instead, constantly judges the government on the basis of the teachings of the Bible. What is more important, they make it clear that we Christians too easily support the injustices of the political-economic system, precisely because that system guarantees that we can have the consumeristic lifestyle that has seduced us all.

The Sojourners Community does not stand alone. It is only a prototype. I know of churches very much like it in cities as large as Chicago and Philadelphia and in towns as small as Americus, Georgia. There are some who estimate that there are hundreds of these groups throughout America, who regularly come together to worship and to strengthen one another to stand against the culture.

Western Christianity very much needs the creative tension created by prophetic countercultural churches such as the Sojourners Community. We need to be challenged by such radical followers of Christ to wake up to what is happening to our people. The prophet of God would probably be happiest in fellowship with them and would resonate most to their message.

The Church of the Oppressed

The problem of racism both inside the Church and in society at large is one the Church in Britain is only now beginning to attempt to get to grips with. In 1991 the Church of England published a report, Seeds of Faith, that pointed ways forward to this most sensitive of issues.

The ecumenical body, the Council of Churches for Britain and Ireland, recently went a step further and issued a hard-hitting call for the Church to help combat racism. The call came from one of the CCBI's presidents, Fr Olu Abiola. He quoted Malachi 3:1–6:

> See, I will send my messenger, who will prepare the way before me. Then suddenly the Lord you are seeking will come to his temple; the messenger of the covenant, whom you desire, will come, says the Lord Almighty.
>
> But who can endure the day of his coming? Who can stand when he appears? For he will be like a launderer's soap. He will sit as a refiner and purifier of silver; he will purify the Levites and refine them like gold and silver. Then the Lord will have men who will bring offerings in righteousness, and the offerings of Judah and Jerusalem will be acceptable to the Lord, as in days gone by, as in former years.
>
> So I will come near to you for judgment. I will be quick to testify against sorcerers, adulterers and perjurers, against those who defraud labourers of their wages, who oppress the widows and the fatherless, and deprive aliens of justice, but do not fear me, says the Lord Almighty.

Father Abiola then said: "God made particular mention of the people he expected would be poor – strangers, widows and orphans. In this context the Church is guilty and continues to be guilty for we see justice is not being done to those who are black." Focusing on the Church, he pointed out that the CCBI is also to challenge racism within its walls and not just in society at large. "We are taught to love your neighbour as yourself and to do unto others as we would do unto ourselves. But how can you say you love God whom you cannot see, and don't love me, whom you can?''

CCRJ moderator, the Rev. Theo Samuel added: ''The Church must be enabled to listen to the black communities as they seek to express the pain of living in a society where their experience is one of inequality and injustice based on racial discrimination.''

And he's right. It's a challenge the Church and Christians ignore at their peril. In that sense it's just like America, which is still reeling from the Los Angeles riots in 1992 after the controversial Rodney King video and verdict and then held its collective breath when Spike Lee's much-hyped and self-titled film of sixties radical Malcolm X was released six months later.

Just as British Afro-Caribbeans drew their inspiration for Gospel music from across the Atlantic after listening to such influential artists as the Rev. James Cleveland, Andrae Crouch and Edwin Hawkins, so, too, have they looked at churches in the States before developing their own uniquely British style of worshp and social interaction. In this regard they have developed more or less independent of the already established white churches, which by and large welcomed them with crossed – not open – arms when they arrived from the Caribbean in the 1950s.

As yet, though, there is no British equivalent to the fiery and controversial New York preacher the Rev. Al Sharpton, who was so memorably satirized as the Rev. Bacon in Tom Wolfe's 1980s novel *The Bonfire of the Vanities*. Sharpton's strength is that he is perceived as the voice of a disenfranchized people, and as such, like him or loathe him, he commands respect. One wonders whether there would have been the Brixton or Toxteth riots in the early 1980s if there had been an Al Sharpton-type around to whom alienated black people could look to accurately voice their grievances before they rioted and looted out of sheer frustration.

Let's look closer at the American model, for there is another church there that stands apart from the social system and challenges its sins. It also would attract the prophet. It stands apart from society not by choice but because it has been pushed there by the people of the ruling establishment. This, of course, is the church of the oppressed. It is the church that gathers together the socially disinherited and gives them a voice.

As a teenager growing up in America, some of my African-American schoolmates took me to the Mount Olive Baptist Church in Philadelphia to hear their preacher, Marshall Shepard, Sr. I had not experienced his kind of preaching before. What he had to say that morning seemed more related to the existential situation of blacks in America than any other sermon I had heard before. He talked of Shadrach, Meshach, and Abednego, these ancient Jewish youths who, while in slavery, refused to bend to the pressures and demands of their masters. Even now I can hear him explaining how these Old Testament heroes, when told to give up the names given to them by their ancestors, refused to do so. They refused, said Shepard, even though it meant being thrown into "the fiery furnace". He rhetorically asked from his pulpit:

Can you imagine those young men being willing to die rather than give up the names of their fathers? Can you understand these young men who would sooner die than to give up who they really were and to forget where they had originally come from? Can you identify with these slaves who would not surrender their identities nor adopt for themselves the last names of their masters?

There were shouts of "Yes!" and "All right now!" All over the congregation there were people becoming aware that

God's people must not deny who they are or ever capitulate to a culture that really is not their own. The people in that Sunday morning congregation were finding in Shepard's message the Biblical support for their efforts to reaffirm their African heritage and to stand fast against those who would make them into something other than they really were. This was anything but good hermeneutics, and it was not even a fair interpretation of what really happened in the Bible story, but it certainly was good preaching!

The climax of Shepard's sermon focused on Moses, and it did so in such a way that it made that Old Testament patriarch a prototype for every African-American man and woman caught up in the identity struggles that go with living in a predominantly white society. He told how Moses, the son of a slave, ended up living in the "big mansion house" of the Pharaoh. He explained how Moses came to be taught the ways of the Egyptians so that he ended up "dressing and talking just like one of them".

But then Shepard went on to relate how, as a young man, Moses came upon an Egyptian soldier beating and kicking a poor, demoralized Jewish slave. Using the vocabulary and idioms of Philadelphia street language, Shepard half shouted and half screamed at the congregation.

But when Moses saw what was happenin' he knew. Somethin' down deep inside told him who he was and where he came from. Somethin' down deep inside made him know that he was one with that Jew and "the Man" – you know what I mean – I mean "the Man" – you know – the man with the whip – that Egyptian man who always is out there making life hard for you – that man – is the enemy, and has to die.

The congregation was alive with shouts of agreement. Some

were clapping. Others were shouting. There were cries for the preacher to "Go on now!"

Everyone there knew that he was talking not just about a Hebrew man who had lived thousands of years ago. They knew he was talking about each of them and what was going on in their own lives. There, in that church, there was little doubt about what the preacher was telling his people to do and be. And being the only white person in that two-thousand-plus gathering, I was more than a bit uncomfortable.

Jesus As a "Nigger"

While Black Liberation Theology can be heard in some form or another from most African-American pulpits, it has gained its best-known expression in the preaching and writing of James Cone. I got a first-hand taste of Cone's message and what he could do to an audience when I once heard him speak at a chapel service at a small Christian college. The predominantly white audience had come with wary anticipation, having heard of Cone's reputation. They sat in dead silence as this teacher in the field of black theology took the rostrum. With his eyes flashing and his voice raised, Cone started his sermon with a line designed to shock them:

"Jesus is a nigger!" he shouted. "And all who would be His followers must be ready to become niggers, too."

The impact was electric. The mostly white audience sat stunned at what had sounded like blasphemy and was, in the minds of most, certainly obscenity. But Cone went on to clarify his statement and to leave most of us convinced that he was right. He explained that, if what we mean by "nigger" is not just a black person, but rather one who is despised, rejected, spat upon, and treated like trash . . . then Jesus was a nigger. The fifty-third chapter of Isaiah, he claimed, said as much.

There was little room for argument when he finished his explanation. Few rebuttals could be offered. There was an obvious biblical basis for his claims. There was only a stunned acceptance of what he had dared to say.

It is not just black theologians who declare that to be a Christian is to identify with the Christ, who Himself identified with the wretched and oppressed of the world. It is not just Cone who would argue that to follow Jesus is to join in the struggle to throw off the chains of inferiority and humiliation and to become part of a movement that brings dignity to all peoples. To be a Christian, many would say, is to join in a revolution. And if that revolution turns violent, it will be the violence of the oppressors who want to "keep black people in their place" that sets off the spark. To the likes of Cone, the time of quiet endurance is over, the time of silent suffering is over. The day of the Lord is at hand!

Women as Oppressed Christians

We need not go to minority groups to find a people with whom a prophet can identify. There is a group of oppressed people *within* the mainstream of Christianity that is beginning to rise up in righteous indignation against the Church and against society. I am referring to women.

Until the last decade, women in the Church did not see themselves as a persecuted group. But all of that has changed. Today there is a growing consciousness among women that they have been denied fair treatment and equality by the male-dominated hierarchies of Christendom. They are rejecting inferior status and the traditional roles that have been assigned to them and are challenging the system with angry demands that things be changed.

In our consumer-oriented, male-chauvinistic society, women have generally been defined as shoppers. Men have been the ones who make the money and their wives, the ones who spend it. Thorsten Veblen, one of the dominant thinkers in sociology and economics in the early part of this century, pointed out that, in America, men were so busy making money that they had no time to spend it. Consequently, men could not buy those things that would signal to others their successful status. That is one reason, said Veblen, that men needed wives. Wives could be "the conspicuous consumers," as he called them, and could buy and parade the clothes, cars, and decorated homes that would show off how successful their husbands had become.

I do not dimiss the Veblen thesis lightly. There is no doubt in my mind that the West has tended to force a definition upon women that has them thinking of themselves primarily as consumers. If the consumer-oriented society is one in which people think that what is really important in life comes with buying things, then women were the first to be duped into this mentality.

Millard Fuller, the founder of Habitat for Humanity, tells of having become a millionaire by the age of twenty-nine. He had, he says, bought his wife "everything" she possibly could want. But one day he came home to a note that announced that she had left him.

Millard went after her and caught up with her on a Saturday night in a hotel in New York City. They talked into the early hours of the next morning as she poured out her heart and made him see that the "things" that our consumer-oriented society says are supposed to be so satisfying had left her cold. Her heart was empty and her spirit was burned out, she explained. She was dead inside and she wanted to live again. Kneeling at their bedside in that hotel room, Millard and Linda decided to sell everything they had and dedicate themselves to serving the poor people and to working for justice for the oppressed.

The next day being Sunday, they found the nearest Baptist

church and went there to worship and thank God for their
new beginning. They got to church early, hunted up the
minister, and told him about what had happened to them
and the decision they had made.

To their surprise, the minister told them that such a radical
decision was not really necessary. "He told us that it was not
necessary for us to give up everything," Millard said. "He
just didn't understand that we weren't giving up money and
the things that money could buy. We were giving up a whole
way of life that was killing us."

Today the Fullers are two of the most alive people I know.
As they work toward making affordable housing available for
the poor, they do so with boundless energy. They have
broken the psychic spell that American consumerism puts on
people. They have "mounted up like eagles". In a hotel room
in New York, they were "born again".

I tell this story because I believe it is symptomatic of what
is happening more and more across the country, and especially
within our churches. Women are rising up and letting it be
known that having store accounts and a credit card is not
enough for them. They are crying out for a chance to invest
their lives in ways that have spiritual significance. They are
demanding the opportunity to do those things that take away
the deadness of their souls. They will no longer tolerate the
numbness of the spirit that comes from being without heroic
options to live out.

The women's movement in the Church is much more than
a crusade to gain the right of ordination for women (although
this is symbolic of what it is all about). It is more than an
attempt to get inclusive language into hymn books. And it
transcends the demand of women to control their biological
destinies. It is a call for liberation from what the Church and
society have done to them. It is an attack on all those cultural
barriers to the full realization of their humanity. Women will

not be satisfied with equal pay for equal work (although they will settle for nothing less). Their aspirations for life cannot be bought off with mink coats and a Mercedes.

In reality the women's movement in the Church is a rebellion against what our consumer-oriented society is all about. That, of course, is why the women's movement is so important to the Church. As women explode the myths of our culture and show us what is of ultimate significance, they stand a chance of dragging the rest of us along with them. We may go kicking and screaming, but we will go, nevertheless.

What women will gain in their struggle for cultural liberation will not only bless them — it will bless all of us male chauvinists who have given them such a hard time and called them degrading names. It just may be that the revival that the Church needs if it is to challenge the psychic slavery and deadness of our culture will come from women. The prophet who delivers us from our consumer-oriented mind-set could well be a prophetess.

Chapter 7

Some Old Wine in Some New Wineskins

Many, if not most, of those who go to church are on a personal survival course. The spiritual death of the nation may be a serious problem, and the need for a prophetic call to repentance may be a crucial necessity, but so many in the Sunday morning congregation have other concerns. They are trying to hold themselves and their families together. Some are struggling to keep empty-shell marriages from falling apart. Others are worried about their alienated kids who are dressing punk and probably doing drugs. There are divorced mothers whose angry children seem out of control. And then there is the man whose alcoholic wife is drinking herself to death. Such people are ready to leave to others the job of assisting at the rebirth of a nation. The wretched poor of the world may desperately need their help, but their own spiritual poverty and the emotional needs of those who are closest to them are what overwhelms most churchgoers. They do not want a church that challenges them to change the world. Instead, they are looking for a church that will comfort them and bind up their wounds. They come to church weary and ready to cry, and they want help.

The more I look at the Church, the more I see an organization run on middle-management multinational principles, but its resemblance to what Jesus envisaged seems coincidental rather than an integral part of its ministry. There's a church I know which once proposed to build an extension so it could meet the needs of its parishioners better. When I pointed out the increasing numbers of homeless people living in the surrounding streets I asked whether the church building would have room for, say, a soup kichen. "Oh no," came the reply, "we can't have down-and-outs messing up our new carpets."

Is the Church to be a great big social centre, where Christians go to chat up and date fellow believers in some sort of holy huddle, or is it the Body of Christ, rolling its sleeves up, unafraid to get its hands and feet dirty and partaking in the world's pain, thereby bringing God into the centre of people's misery, unhappiness and confusion? Instead we're surrounded by a Jesus Junk culture, where we're so obsessed with so many personal spiritual self-improvement programmes that we miss the point. "Whatever you did for one of the least of these brothers of mine," Jesus said, "you did for me." And he wasn't pointing to that squeaky-clean Christian club, the Church-a-Go-Go, where everyone present assumes they're the only one having a hard time there for all the others look so, so successful.

Rather, Jesus was referring to those who aren't plump and well fed, those reduced to drinking their own urine for they have no other source of liquid refreshment, those alienated either from themselves or dispossessed for no fault of their own, those whose clothes do not hide their nakedness and vulnerability underneath, those so ill they cannot help themselves even if they wanted to, and those trapped within prisons, be they physical with iron bars, or bodies that have ceased to function, or within their own minds.

These are the people of whom Jesus said that if we lose the point: "I tell you the truth, whatever you did not do for one of the least of these, you did not do for me" (Matthew 25:44). Hard words, hard truth. But luckily we are not called to do things alone, even though so much church-based activity puts this contradictory message across by keeping personal piety just that, personal. There are many Christian people and organizations around which share similar concerns to God even if your church doesn't.

One such is UNLEASH, United London Ecumenical Action on Single Homelessness. As of September 1991 it estimated there were some 300,000 homeless people in the capital alone. This represents a staggering 78,000 homeless single people and 88,000 homeless families (assuming each has an average 2.5 members). Of these, 2000 to 3000 are sleeping rough in the streets – the tip of a giant iceberg – with 9000 squatting and 19,000 in night shelters and hostels.

I asked Southwark diocesan housing adviser Pat Logan what we should do if approached for money in the street. Do we give it or shy away? "There is no easy or general answer," Pat replies. "I would first of all go by how the person looked, their general physical appearance, to determine how well they were, and then talk to them to find out their condition. Sometimes you see people who are almost blue with cold. In that situation you might ask if they'd like a cup of coffee or something. They might say, 'Get lost!' or 'You're the first person who has stopped to talk to me'.

"There're no rules. You can't be sure. Some may have no money and be very vulnerable, while others may have a hostel bed but know this particular patch is a good one to be given money at. I don't mean to sound cynical, but if you become used to this way of life you get to know the ropes."

Pat Logan specializes in working with single homeless in south London. He also works for UNLEASH and urges Christians, whether individually or as a church, to get more involved with the issue. However, he points out, the motivation must not be a sense of guilt but rather one of love for these people because they too are made in the image of God. But, he adds, don't be surprised if your concern for their wellbeing is misunderstood and gets thrown back in your face. "You can't solve the problem by taking the person into a café for a meal. Whatever you do, giving money or buying a meal is not a solution. But don't be too bothered about making 'wrong' decisions either. Don't adopt an iron-clad rule – 'I'll never give money to these people because there are some dishonest ones'. What does it matter? It's only a few pounds anyway."

But the churches are finally waking up and being mobilized into action over this particular issue. In 1991 the Churches National Housing Coalition, an ecumenical pressure group, was formed and on 1 December 1992 over 2000 Christians representing churches the length and breadth of the country lobbied Parliament about the issue. "There has been a lot of concern in churches about the plight of homeless people and a lot of people want to do something," Pat says. "If a church wants to do something, the best place to start is its own area. Make some enquiries. Most towns have a Housing Advice Centre. See if, either as an individual or as a church group or PCC (Parish Church Council), you can get someone from the Housing Advice Centre to talk about the people who are coming to them and the needs that exist in a particular borough.

"Try to find out what's going on already and see if you can support that by providing volunteers, transport, with a lodging scheme – there's a whole range of those that might need committee members, money and blankets."

Jesus said in Matthew: "The poor you will always have with you . . .", but this has been taken to mean that God somehow wants to reinforce this social status quo. If there will always be poor people, the faulty logic goes, why bother to help them?

Fi McLachlan, formerly director of Homeless Projects for the Oasis Trust, says this is a distortion of what the Bible means. "In the Old Testament God didn't give laws to the Israelites that said, 'Be extra nice to those who are well off and live in palaces', but he did make a point of telling them to welcome the stranger in and let them off their debts, because he felt it was really important to say that."

Pat Logan agrees. It's not enough for the Government to become increasingly reliant on Christian and voluntary organizations to pick up the pieces of lives crushed by the wheels of bureaucracy. Rather, he says, important questions must be asked. "It's important to reflect on what's going on, and why. Why are there homeless people whom we're trying to help? Possibly there's a blockage in the system. What causes it? What is the Church's responsibility as a church?

"Really it's a question of thinking out the theology – not in an academic way – with some Christian reflection of the experience of being homeless."

Church Action on Poverty, in conjunction with the campaigning charity Shelter, has produced Windows and Walls, an excellent guide to homelessness, putting it into a social context. It is a valuable document in helping to develop a theological underpinning of the issue and how to respond Christianly. As Fi says: "God's heart is inclusive. He doesn't want people to be ostracized, marginalized, pushed out and, these days, left on the streets. Reading the Bible with an eye on what he said about homes, I realized afresh how much Scripture talks about the heart God has for people on the outside, the outcasts.

"And Jesus teaches that as much as we're doing it for the weakest we're doing it to him, like Mother Teresa, who talks about ministering to the poor as ministering to Jesus. We cannot escape that if we care to look, but so often we choose not to because it means upsetting our lifestyle, our time schedules, our finances and opening our church halls. So it's uncomfortable for Christians to make a response."

And there's the rub. If it's uncomfortable for Christians to put their hands into their pockets, then how much more uncomfortable is it for those living on the streets? It's not about going to a politically correct and ideologically "right on" church that makes us feel good, but rather in following Christ. Then there's the phrase "the image of God" that rolls so glibly off our tongues. What exactly does it mean when we describe fellow human beings this way, especially the ones who in the words of Liverpudlian poet Roger McGough, "aimed low in life and missed"?

"Do we really see God's image in a homeless person?" Pat Logan asks. "What we need to talk about is who the last person I saw on the street was. Male or female? How old? What did he or she look like? How did I feel? It's teasing out the meaning of that experience, so part of that theology could well be how the image of God becomes the overriding way in which I approach the homeless. I could also feed back into questions like, 'why is the Church and its resources where they are?'

"Where does the issue of homelessness fit in time-wise in our Church? Should we be grateful that in the 1980s homelessness took up more of the Church's time than ever before? Is that our benchmark – isn't it wonderful what we're doing now? – or should it be what's the overall mission of the Church and how far are we from being the kind of Church we're required to be? I'm not trying to say the right answer is to put homelessness on the top of the agenda. It's not as simple as that. These are theological questions about our wider world – not just homelessness, but our prayer life, our worship, our overall resources, whom we train and what we talk about as Christians."

If people treat you as trash, then that's how you'll come to see yourself as being. As Fi McLachlan observes: "Some people think homeless people are scum because they're begging on the streets. But what we don't understand is that they've been knocked around for the past ten years, the family split up, there's nowhere to go, and they didn't have friends and a nice church to support them. They're like you and me – only they've had different life experiences and have neither been loved nor cared for. I don't feel we've any room to make judgments about these people. Before God we're all the same. Just because we've got nice clothes and a nice house, God doesn't care any more about us than a person begging on the street.

"Oasis believes the Gospel means the whole Gospel – meeting people's needs as whole people. Jesus met people's physical needs first of all. He gave bread to people who were hungry. He didn't say, 'I will only feed those who come to the front and repent'. He met people where they were at. On the street, to tell people the Gospel is really Good News and that it will change their lives isn't going to cut any ice with them when they are saying, 'I'm hungry, I need a roof over my head, I need help'. We need to start there, caring for them in a practical way. Jesus was an example of that."

Truly it is only through losing our lives that we find them. Spirituality is about service to others, not what we can get out of life for ourselves. We would do well to remember this next Sunday as we sit in our favourite pew.

People need personal salvation. They need a personal mystical oneness with the resurrected Christ. They need the psychological wholeness and the emotional wellbeing that accompanies becoming new persons in Christ. However, the God of the Bible not only concerns Himself with establishing a personal saving relationship with His Son but also is committed to social justice for all the peoples of the world. The biblical Jesus not only is desperate to help lost sinners "find themselves" but also wills to express the righteousness of Heaven in the context of those social institutions wherein we must live our lives.

> But when Jesus [knew the Pharisees were plotting against him], he withdrew himself from thence: and great multitudes followed him, and he healed them all;
> And charged them that they should not make him known:
> That it might be fulfilled which was spoken by Isaiah the prophet, saying,
> Behold my servant, whom I have chosen; my beloved, in whom my soul is well pleased: I will put my Spirit upon him, and he shall show judgment to the Gentiles.
> He shall not strive, nor cry; neither shall any man hear his voice in the streets.
> A bruised reed shall he not break, and smoking flax shall he not quench, till he send forth judgment unto victory.
> And in his name shall the Gentiles trust.
>
> Matthew 12:15–21

Mid-Range Ways in a Great Big Church

I think that even many of the "successful" churches are beginning to do some things that could change them significantly. I am referring to the fact that, in many of them, people are becoming involved in mid-range efforts to affect the world for Christ.

For instance, Holy Trinity, Brompton does a lot of work amongst London's homeless people and others who may be down but are by no means out. Called the Earl's Court Project and based in west London, it holds meetings for the homeless, people with AIDS, and prostitutes. This was opened several years ago in conjunction with Youth with a Mission and Christian AIDS charity ACET. From this has developed the

Arbour, a safe house in Clapham, south London, for people
wanting to break free of addictive lifestyles.

Again, in America, home of the superchurches, some with
literally thousands of members and apparently limitless
resources, are starting to move in this socially aware direction.
In Hollywood, California, just off the famous corner of
Hollywood and Vine, one of these superchurches has
established a ministry to teenage runaways, prostitutes and
street people.

A few young adults from the church have moved into a
house that they open up to the hurting people who hang out
at this world-famous corner. They provide counselling,
temporary housing, and prayer. These dedicated young
people are just a handful of a colossal congregation, but I
think they have a chance of being a sector that could begin
to stir the rest of the church to a new vision of what the
church should be about.

In nearby Newport Beach, the youth programme of another
superchurch involves getting teenagers to work in ministries
in the slums of Tijuana and in the island nation of Haiti. It
may not seem like much in the grand scheme of the
multiplicity of programmes sponsored by this particular
superchurch, but it could sensitize the young people and help
to break the false consciousness that characterizes people in
this consumer-oriented society.

In Atlanta, Georgia, there is a superchurch that has a good
number of its men working regularly with Habitat for
Humanity. The impact of this involvement is beginning to
show its effects in the overall life of the church. One of the
men told me that his work with Habitat was as significant
as his "born-again" experience when he first came to know
about the salvation of Christ. "My work with Habitat has
got me on fire," he told me. "Being a Christian has a whole
new meaning to me now."

Such instances may not seem to amount to much when we see how few of the people in the mega-churches are involved in them and how little of the money in the multimillion-dollar budgets of those churches is involved. But remember, the Kingdom of God is a Mustard Seed Conspiracy. There's no telling what God can do through such small beginnings. Something as old as the new life preached by the prophets may, through these mid-range efforts, become a transforming influence on a lot of people in the prosperous established churches and in the new superchurches that are being born across America.

Chapter 8

Making It Happen on Broad Street

North Philadelphia contains one of the worst black ghettos in America. Hundreds of thousands of people live in dilapidated houses owned by landlords. Violent crime is commonplace, as drug cartels compete to control the lucrative trade in "crack" and 'ice". Most people are afraid to venture out after dark, and the police who walk the streets are filled with fear. During the daytime hours, children play on wasteground strewn with discarded rubbish and junked cars. Teenagers skipping school seem omnipresent. Unemployment in this rundown area is hard to figure; estimates run as high as 40 per cent. Storekeepers are closing their businesses because they have been robbed too often and no longer want a daily existence that is fraught with the fear of violence and death.

But in the midst of this dying ghetto, something incredible is happening. A Pentecostal church is growing by leaps and bounds. This church is committed to doing what many might consider impossible – rebuilding the community. Having begun as a storefront church, Deliverance Tabernacle on North Broad Street has steadily and dramatically increased its membership and now holds services in what previously had been one of Philadelphia's largest movie houses. Thousands squeeze in to the Sunday morning services to participate in exuberant worship. Emotions are released and ecstasy expressed in ways that represent the best of the African-American experience.

The excitement of Deliverance Tabernacle does not end with Sunday morning worship. In reality, what happens on Sunday is only a launching pad for a variety of social activities that are earning an impressive list of successes in the North Philadelphia area. Not only does this church provide an array of helping services such as legal counselling, medical care, and recreational schemes, but it has embarked on an ambitious plan to redevelop the living conditions and the economy of the surrounding neighbourhood.

Deliverance Tabernacle has organized and trained young people to rehabilitate deserted houses, which in that part of the city number in the thousands. Through this, not only are jobs being created for a lot of teenagers, but inexpensive housing is being offered for sale to many poor people. The church provides a "total care" programme that involves housing, feeding, and caring for elderly people in the community, many of whom previously had lived alone in dingy rat-infested flats.

The most impressive venture of Deliverance has been its success in developing a new shopping centre complete with a supermarket, a bank, and a variety of small businesses, including a fast-food outlet. In this shopping centre young men and women are learning how to be shop assistants. Unemployed residents of the area are finding work, and people from blocks around are discovering a good place to shop. Previously, the disintegration of the neighbourhood had made such opportunities and services increasingly rare. But with the daring and hard work of the members of Deliverance Tabernacle, this trend has been reversed. The shopping centre is doing what many thought could not be done. It is rejuvenating the area. It is creating new life where there had been only social decline. Deliverance Tabernacle is initiating what Hebraic scholars call "Shalom" and what Christian theologians call the "Kingdom of God".

Experts in city renewal come from all over the country to see what this church is pulling off. But what has happened under the auspices of Deliverance Tabernacle can hardly be replicated by governments on the city or state levels. This began as a grassroots operation and has been generated out of small groups of people who not only learned to work together but also learned how to pray together.

The ministry of Deliverance Tabernacle is wholly related to the beliefs and practices of its congregation. Every activity has been undergirded with prayer. Every administrator has come to his or her position with a sense of having been "called" and ordained by God. All the important decisions that have gone into making these projects successful have been the subjects of long prayer meetings by the people. In so many ways, what has been happening in North Philadelphia through the people of Deliverance Tabernacle is the work of the Holy Spirit.

Deliverance Tabernacle's membership is large enough for it to be considered a superchurch. But it breaks the patterns of most superchurches in that it understands that part of its mission is to change the world and not just to help troubled people to live successful lives in the world that is. Undoubtedly, the mission of Deliverance Tabernacle, in part, comes out of its people. As African-Americans, the members of Deliverance Tabernacle have endured humiliation and oppression from the dominant middle-class white society. They know that such a society must be changed and that they themselves must be a countercultural force helping to make that happen.

Mid-Range Projects Affect the Life of the Church

The reason for focusing on the work of Deliverance Tabernacle is not simply to tell about another grassroots effort to effect social change. What I want to talk about is what has happened to the people of Deliverance Tabernacle in the process of engaging in these social ministries. While what these people have been doing is a blessing to the neighbourhood, what I want you to see is that their activities have had an incredible influence on what has been going on in their own personal lives and in the life of their church. The benefits these projects have reaped for the church people who have brought them about are more than worth the cost that the church has had to pay in carrying them out. They have given to the people of Deliverance a whole new quality of spirituality.

First of all, there is the effect that this outreach has had on the young people of the church. As they have organized to carry out various responsibilities connected with these projects, they have developed an intense closeness. They have become best friends. From the beginning, these young people have spent most of their spare time together. They have become, in the words of sociologist Charles Cooley, a "primary group". Their intense relationships have served to reinforce the Christian values they had learned at church and have helped to give them clear personal identities.

Living as they do, in a social environment that is both anti-Christian and delinquent, it is nearly impossible for most teenagers and young adults in an area like this to stand alone and to withstand the pressures to conform. But with the constant reinforcing of Christian values and the regular revitalization of the identity that has come from participation in their youth group at Deliverance Tabernacle, these young people have gained the wherewithal to stand firm. The relationships developed in social action through the church have given them the fortitude and courage to maintain a Christian counterculture mentality in the midst of a very tough environment. Were this not the case, the dominant society would probably have swallowed them up and enculturated them into its own image. Instead, these primary groups, formed to carry out assignments related to the Church's neighbourhood development projects, have made these young people more than able to survive as a "peculiar people" (I Peter 2:9).

All of this only heightens our awareness of the need to create small groups of Christians who will work together to do the work of the Kingdom. Such groups create what biblical scholars call *koinonia*, a special kind of fellowship that belongs to those who feel spiritual oneness in Christ.

Groups that get together simply to ensure their own survival rarely last. But when a group has a mission that carries it beyond its own self-interest, its members usually find that their common mission cements them together. More important, we should note that it is only in the context of such intensely committed groups that a countercultural value system can be maintained and a clear understanding of what it means to be a radical Christian established.

Peter Berger, one of America's most popular contemporary sociologists, gives a great deal of attention to this process of identity reinforcement within a primary group. Berger contends that, in order to maintain a consciousness that is other than that prescribed by the dominant society, the individual must be part of what he calls a "plausibility structure". This is a small group that serves to keep individuals from coming to think that they are crazy or that their beliefs are unreal. According to Berger, the only way that a person can go on believing that a countercultural belief system is viable is by having it regularly revitalized within a plausibility structure that shares that belief system.

A Way to Be Filled with the Spirit

Evangelical Christians, particularly of the Charismatic stripe, have come to discover some supernatural benefits from such small-group relationships. These benefits far transcend what sociologists can observe empirically. Christians are discovering that in small groups that are committed to Christian mission, there is often a mystical encounter with the power and presence of the Holy Spirit. While I am not attempting here to spell out the whys and wherefores of how the Holy Spirit works in the world, I am suggesting that the most "normal" way to experience the Spirit is in the context of small-group relationships. I believe that this is what Jesus was getting at when He said, "For where two or three are gathered together in my name, there am I in the midst of them" (Matthew 18:20). I believe that somehow the Holy Spirit chooses to emerge in a special way when small groups of Christians interact meaningfully and intensely. I believe that the Holy Spirit comes *through* the others to the individual and *through* the individual to the others.

Jesus Himself had such a support group. It was composed of Peter, James, and John. Whenever there were to be high times of spiritual ecstasy, such as on the Mount of Transfiguration (Mark 9:2–12), these three were chosen to be with Him. He loved the twelve, but these three were special. He took them away from the others to pray with great regularity.

As the Son of Man, as Jesus liked to call Himself, He was in *need* of the renewal of the Spirit that could come in the context of the intense prayer and fellowship that He shared with His small company of disciples. That, of course, is what made Gethsemane so painful for Him. It appears that in the hour when He most needed the spiritual revitalization that comes from such mutual intimacy in the Spirit, His support group fell asleep on Him, leaving Him to struggle with His painful destiny alone.

What Jesus sought in His small prayer group is, in a limited way, what the young people of Deliverance Tabernacle found in their small groups. And from a sociological perspective, that small-group experience is the primary means for maintaining a lifestyle of nonconformity in a world in which being a Christian is often countercultural. At a time in Western Christianity when people want to *experience* God, not just believe in Him, such small-group encounters become increasingly important to the Christian lifestyle that is meaningful to them.

Serving as though People Matter

So often, social schemes designed by government agencies fail to take into consideration the people being served. Those who come up with grand schemes for society often overlook the concerns of individuals. Macro programmes are usually carried out by "experts" who assume they know what people need more than the people themselves do. Certainly this was the case when, in the late fifties and early sixties, the governments in Britain and America attempted to address the need for low-cost housing. Architects, social workers, and government officials were involved in the planning and building of high-rise buildings to house poor people who, for the most part, were either low-paid workers or unemployed.

Nobody asked the people who would have to live in these flats what they wanted. Consequently, when these buildings were erected, they proved to be dysfunctional. Children out playing were not about to take a lift up twenty floors to go to the toilet. The way in which the buildings were constructed kept neighbours from getting to know each other, and the hallways of many of these buildings proved to be unsafe late at night. These high-rise blocks are now seen as a mistake and are being pulled down in many places.

There are a host of other examples of how urban planners

and government social workers, for all their good intentions, often fail in their efforts simply because they do not listen to the people whom they are trying to serve.

The opposite was true of those who developed the social ministries of Deliverance Tabernacle. The Deliverance projects have been carried out by people who knew the residents of the community. Actually, most of them were residents of the area and talked constantly to their neighbours about the things that their church was trying to do. Small grassroots groups have a sensitivity to neighbourhood sentiments that official planners can never have. That is why projects designed and executed by small groups of people working on the community level are far more effective than those that are planned and carried out by women and men who sit in offices of power at city or county hall.

As Deliverance Tabernacle members carried out their church's plans for community development, many of them learned new ways to relate effectively to their neighbours and community leaders. As individuals they developed self-confidence. They overcame the reluctance that sometimes keeps people from confrontations over points of difference. They learned how to develop a community consensus on difficult issues.

A side effect that few people expected when these social service projects were first initiated was a significant evangelistic outreach for the church. The discussions with neighbours about what the church was doing and the possible consequences of these efforts on the community opened the doors for discussion about Christ and what He wills for the world. Many who at first were only interested in what the projects would do for or to the community were soon involved in deep spiritual discussions about Christ and the Kingdom of God. Several who wanted to participate in making the neighbourhood a more decent place in which to live were soon drawn into the life of the church and into a personal commitment to the Gospel.

Additionally, the various projects of Deliverance Tabernacle gave new meaning to the prayer life of the church. Elderly shut-ins now spend long hours praying for those in positions of leadership and asking for divine intervention as difficult barriers and problems arise. Weekly midweek prayer meetings at church are now well attended as people of the church come to lean on Jesus for help and guidance. Participants in these projects sense that the work they have to do is too much for them to handle alone, and they have learned to go to the Lord in prayer. The vitality of the prayer life of Deliverance Tabernacle has increased dramatically as a result of the church's community involvement through its people.

I tell the story of Deliverance Tabernacle because I believe the things this church is doing and the ways in which its people are being changed are examples of what has to happen all over if the Western world is to be saved. I believe that if people in cities, towns, and villages would be mobilized into community-based efforts to solve pressing problems and to meet human needs, then there could be a new beginning for us all.

Praxis Lived Out

Sociologists use the term *praxis* to refer to the belief that people are changed by what they do. But they do not mean pure activism when they talk of praxis. They are referring to something far deeper. Praxis is action in reflection and/or reflection in action. It is a special kind of thinking that takes place when people are actually doing things. People do one kind of thinking when they read or discuss ideas. They do another kind of thinking when they are involved in trying to change the world. The first kind of thinking is the prerogative of scholars. The second takes place in the minds of those who are caught up in an intense struggle to solve the problems that are part of their everyday lives as they try to earn a living, raise a family, fight crime in their community, and make their schools responsive to the needs of their children. The first kind of thinking creates opinions that can be changed. The second kind forms convictions that change those who think that way.

What has being going on at Deliverance Tabernacle has been praxis. People are not just doing things; they are being changed by what they do. The false consciousness perpetrated by their consumer-oriented society is being broken, and they are seeing the world in a new light. Their struggles in trying to carry out their mid-range programmes for social change have brought about a new frame of mind. What is important to them, how they view themselves, and what they think their lives are all about have all changed. God is doing a new thing among them. They are coming alive. They are people with a new vision. They are a people filled with new dreams.

I have talked to them. I have watched the eyes of their youth flash with excitement. I have seen older people demonstrate the energy of fleet-footed deer. I have seen what prophets have always hoped would happen to people actually taking place in these small beginnings.

It is embryonic. It is small. It is like a mustard seed. But there is new life there. There is something that could be a foretaste of a new society.

A Theory of Social Change

Many would go along with my claims that the mid-range activities of the people at Deliverance Tabernacle have done them a lot of good. But sceptics and doomsayers would go on to say that, while such things can get people "feeling good", the social system itself will remain unchanged.

It reminds me of an excellent cartoon called Pontius' Puddle by American cartoonist Joel Kaufmann that I saw recently in the Church of England Newspaper. The first of the two-box strip showed Pontius the frog praying and asking God, "I'd like to work for peace on Earth, Lord, but what can one person do?" The second box shows our planet with lots of speech bubbles dotted around it, all asking the same question, "What can one person do?"

Think of the world and all its global problems – wars, and rumours of wars, widespread famine and mass starvation, collapsing economies and rampant inflation, millions living in squalor and abject poverty while millions more live in affluence and almost decadence – while much closer to home we have nuclear families disintegrating at an increasing rate as divorce seems set to be the rule rather than the exception in Western society. And the gap between North and South seems wider than that of the rich man and Lazarus in Jesus' parable. What can one person do? Indeed.

Think globally and your mind freezes. Instead think locally. Look around your street, the neighbourhood where you live, and now ask yourself, "What can one person do?" Not as much perhaps as ten or twenty all motivated by the Gospel to take Christ to poor, oppressed and hurting people. One thread can easily be broken. But try snapping a thick rope composed of tightly-bound threads. As the well-known chorus goes, "Bind us together with bonds that cannot be broken . . . Bind us together in love."

Alexis de Tocqueville saw that such local, community-based ventures were what made society work. Back in the early nineteenth century, de Tocqueville made it clear that the diffusion of democracy in a thousand town meetings for the planning and creating of schools, hospitals, and fire companies was what made people alive and dynamic. More contemporary social scientists like Robert Nisbet, Peter

Berger, and Talcott Parsons would say the same thing. *Small is Beautiful* could be more than a title of a book. It could easily be the slogan for this style of social change, which I believe could bring new hope and life to our people.

If the last couple of decades have taught us anything, they should have taught us that trying to change the structure of society from the top down does not work very well. During the Reagan/Thatcher years there was much talk about supply-side economics and trickle-down economic theory. The word coming out of Washington and Downing Street then was an up-to-date version of the old line, "What's good for General Motors is good for the country." In more direct terms, all that meant was that if big business was thriving it would stimulate the development and growth of smaller businesses, and new jobs would be created throughout the social system. The idea was that the smaller businesses have the bigger businesses as customers, so the health of the latter should determine the health of the former.

In many ways the Reagan/Thatcher years provided some startling economic successes. By the end of the period, Britain and America had survived an economic recession and had experienced several "boom" years.

But were things as they seemed? Had big business really saved us? Did the tax cuts and incentives that governments provided for the heavy industries and the big corporations really do the job?

Actually, the answer proved to be "No!" While big businesses provided some stimulation for the development of small businesses, the truth is that things were the other way around. Small businesses were what got big businesses and big industry rolling.

Any analysis of the economic scene during the Reagan/Thatcher years would demonstrate that what really happened was that small entrepreneurs provided the primary job-creating force in America and the UK. From one end of these countries to the other, small businesses and small industries created by a host of enterprising risk-takers were the ones who really put American and British people back to work in record numbers. The people employed by these small businesses and industries had money to spend, and they bought things. And it is when they began buying the likes of cars, television sets, refrigerators and washing machines that the big industries that produced them started doing well. Positive social change occurs on the micro level first. It is there that the forces that make the economy go are unleashed.

This lesson is not going unnoticed in Third-World countries. One by one the poor nations of the world are beginning to abandon their schemes for massive planned economic development and are concentrating on encouraging the development of small cottage industries and small businesses. Operations that involve ten or fifteen people are much more likely to succeed than are massive industries that are, in theory, supposed to create jobs for hundreds or even thousands of workers.

Small businesses, it has been learned, create new jobs at a much lower cost than do large industries. For instance, in a high-tech big business, it may take as much as £50,000 to create a single employment opportunity. A small business can create a new job for as little as £50.

Opportunity International, a Chicago-based Christian missionary organization, grasped this fact and has set up a job creation programme based on it. It has concentrated on providing loans to Third-World entrepreneurs who demonstrate a capacity to start small businesses or cottage industries. The results of Opportunity International have been amazing. Working in forty-six countries, with limited funds, Opportunity International has generated more than thirty-six thousand jobs. It has led the way for a whole new kind of missionary work. Young men and women are regularly signing up to work with this organization, because they are convinced that, by creating these "intermediate units" in Third-World economies, they can be the most effective kinds of agents of social change.

At Eastern College, where we have a graduate programme designed to prepare missionaries to do this kind of development work, I have an easy time convincing students that they are the real hope for the future. I tell them something like this:

You could go into a small city like Cap Haitien, Haiti, and over a decade create forty or sixty small businesses. Assuming that each of these businesses ends up employing ten people, you could be supplying jobs for as many as six hundred families in that city. Knowing, as you do, that people who earn money spend money, you can surmise that the working people who spend what they earn will create still more jobs.

How long do you think that it will be before there is a good educational system in that city? If people have money to pay teachers, don't you think that there will be a decent school fairly soon?

How long do you think it will take to get good medical services there? If people can pay for doctors, don't you think that there will be not only doctors, but hospitals and clinics as well?

How long do you think it will be before there is an adequate food supply in that city? When there is money to buy food, how long do you think it will take before the food is available?

In the end, how long will it be before a democratic political system is called for? If wealth is distributed in an egalitarian fashion through job creation, how long do you

think it will take before there will be a government that
is responsive to the needs of the people?

Of course, things never work out as simply as my speech
suggests. But there is enough truth to the plan to make the
students believe that they can make a difference in the macro
scheme of things by creating mid-range economic units.

The Church as Initiator

Mid-range activity, as a means of recreating society and giving
new life to its people, is more and more being seen as a
redeeming force in our communities. But we all know that
for anything to start on the local level there has to be a
catalyst. There has to be some agency or person from whom
comes initiative, inspiration, and vision. *Enter the Church*! I
am convinced that the Church can play this crucial role. I
believe that the Church was *meant* to play this role. I believe
that it was for such a mission that the Church was created
in the first place. The Church has the value system that can
provide the basis for altruistic service. Sometimes the Church
has lost sight of its biblical imperatives to be a "suffering
servant" for the world and has become as self-interested and
self-contained as any of the worldly institutions that surround
it. But the Bible is always there to tell the Church what it
is supposed to be and do. And more often than its critics are
ready to admit, pastors and preachers call the Church back
to its high calling.

The Church has all that is needed to make mid-range
programmes happen. In its laity are the human resources to
organize community projects and the skills to translate dreams
and visions into concrete reality. The Church also has the
financial resources that are needed for these ventures.

Frequently, the clergy has refused to release church lay

persons for ministry outside the immediate interests of the institutional Church. And more often than those of us in the Church want to admit, the church leaders have kept its wealth to serve only ecclesiastical interests. But there are prophetic voices within the Church that are calling its people to give themselves and all they own away to meet the needs of a needy world. There are Mother Teresa and Bishop Tutu, as well as countless hundreds of others who have not won Nobel prizes, who call for such sacrifices. And their voices *are* being heard.

The Church has the vision that is needed for the rebirth of Western society. That vision is a new humanity, which has been revealed in Jesus Christ. It is the dream of a new society filled with loving responsibility. That vision has been fleshed out in the life of the Christians portrayed in the book of Acts. All that has to happen is for the Church to be The Church and the West will have what it needs to live again.

A Parable for the Church

There was a land where there was a great oil refinery. The refinery was gigantic and was known to employ all the modern techniques of chemical engineering. Its facilities were bright and shining, and those who worked there made sure that everything was kept in good condition and that everything ran well.

One day, some visitors to the land asked to have a tour of the refinery. At first there was reluctance to show the visitors what they wanted to see. But when the visitors insisted the rulers of the land directed that they be given an extensive tour of the refinery.

After seeing the vast chambers for processing petroleum, the gleaming pipes that carried the petroleum products from place to place, and the extensive organizational system that had been set in place to keep the refinery going, the visitors asked to see the shipping department. "What shipping department?" asked the tour guide in response.

"Why, the shipping department from whence you ship out all the gasoline and oil that you process here," said the tourists.

"We don't have any shipping department," answered the guide. "You see, all the energy products produced in this refinery are used up keeping the refinery going."

Sometimes I think that the Church is as absurd as that make-believe refinery. At times it functions in much the same way. I would have to join the critics who say that most of the energy that the Church produces is used up for nothing more than keeping the Church going. Its money and its people are in large measure used up to maintain the institution, and relatively little goes out to meet the needs of the world. That has to change.

At its best, the Church is the only organization that exists solely for the good of its nonmembers. At its best, the Church understands the words of Christ and knows that if it seeks to save itself, it will lose itself, but if it is willing to give itself away to meet the needs of others, it will live. The Church must live up to its calling. A dying civilization and a people who have lost their collective soul are depending on it.

In concrete terms, America, for example, waits for one hundred thousand churches to give away their human and financial resources to build houses for the poor and shelters for street people; organize crusades to save the environment; create jobs for the unemployed; provide help to single mothers, decent education for the socially disinherited, and deliverance for those who are being dehumanized in prison; and do a hundred and one other things that need to be done on the local level by community people. To respond to these needs, churches will have to preach the Gospel to win converts as never before. But these new converts will not be people who "get saved" just so that they can go to heaven. Instead, they will be a people of God, committed to be agents of God's revolution. They will be part of the Mustard Seed Conspiracy composed of mid-range efforts carried out by a people who are coming to life.

Chapter 9

Getting Down Where It Counts

It's up to us. Now. The means of seeing God's will being done on Earth as it is in Heaven is in our hands, in our lives. But we can't do it alone, as much as we'd like to. We need the help of our pastors, church leaders and others in positions of spiritual responsibility, for in some respects they are the ones who hold our destiny in their hands.

If we are going to be challenged as Christians and to challenge others too, we ought to pray for them, that they also will be open to what God would have them do. For though they do such good work, I don't believe the megachurches I mentioned earlier are where God's really going to work in our society and culture. Rather, the smaller, more intimate churches, where you know you're a name and not a number, is where God is especially at work.

However, revival won't come from communities such as the Sojourners either. Though the prophetic message they proclaim is at the heart of what the biblical message is all about, they too lack the contact with the masses which is essential for our new vision and our new future.

This is why we need to pray for ourselves, our fellow church members and our church leaders, that with us they will catch the vision and help to further God's Kingdom on Earth in our homes, on our streets, in our workplaces, in pubs – and in churches. The responsibility is awesome, for this is God's work we're on, and this fact alone ought to cause us sober reflection and contemplation. Those who lead us in worship and head the ministry of God's people have an incredible responsibility, for, as James the Apostle warns, those who teach the Word of God will be held more accountable for what happens to people than anyone else (James 3:1). For this reason alone we ought to pray and intercede for them, that when revival comes they aren't just prepared but are also at the forefront of it.

Concerts of Prayer for Preachers

The validity of what I am saying must be apparent. And yet it sends slight tremors up and down our spines. We hate to admit it, but those who lead our churches do not always inspire us with confidence. Some seem beaten down because of constant criticism and picking that usually comes from members and elders in their churches. Some, overcome by disillusion, have given up on their dreams and settled down to the routines of running an institution. Some have simply lost their "first love" and are spiritually cold (Revelation 2:4). And some are just plain tired.

We need not just sit back, throw up our hands, and resign ourselves to the sorry condition of these discouraged men and women who have been called to lead us. *We can pray*.

You may think that this kind of statement is the sort of cop-out to be expected from somebody who doesn't know what else to say and who has no *practical* suggestions to make. Nothing could be farther from the truth.

In the Bible, prophets arose because the people prayed for God to raise them up. When the children of Israel felt that they were living in a spiritual wasteland, they prayed that God would give them a prophet, and God answered their prayers. In Bible days, the revival of a people and the renewal of the nation always began with prayer. Without prayer there were no prophets.

We do not pay enough attention to how prayer works. Through prayer, God channels His power *through* people *to* people. By that I mean that, through prayer, I can do more than make requests known to God. It is also possible through prayer to make myself available to God to be a conduit through whom His Spirit can flow toward another person. In prayer I can open myself up to be filled with the power of God. Then I can mentally and spiritually direct all of that power toward some person or persons and become a lens through which the light and power of God can be focused onto the lives of others. When I do that, I can sense that God is using me as a means through whom His dynamistic Spirit goes out into the world to affect lives and make miracles happen.

But this does not mean that we can merely sit back and pray that the Holy Spirit prods someone else into action. When we pray we must always be willing to be part of His answer ourselves. We will never be judged on the failures and omissions of others, only our own.

The Strange Experiences of Frank Laubach

But praying for our leaders can have wonderful effect. Frank Laubach, the famous missionary and educator, tells of going into a church on an Easter Sunday morning and finding it a spiritually deadening experience. Instead of accepting things as they were, he decided to be spiritually aggressive. He decided to go at the pastor and the members of the congregation in the power of the Holy Spirit.

First Laubach decided to work on the pastor. He tells how he surrendered himself to the infilling of the Spirit and then directed what he was receiving from God at the man in the pulpit. The effects, said Laubach, were almost immediate and also more than apparent. That preacher's message gradually began to evidence life and vitality. The words of the sermon came alive, and the pastor's entire being seemed to throb with excitement.

Then, according to Laubach, the individuals in the congregation became the subjects of his empowering prayers. One by one, he picked out persons in the congregation and focused the enlivening power of God toward each of them. The results, he contends, were amazing. He tells how he actually saw heads jerk back as he focused on them. It seemed that the Spirit flowing through him was awakening each of them to hear the Gospel. The congregation became every bit as alive as the pastor. Soon an awesome dynamic filled the place, and a spirit of revival was alive in that church.

When the service was over, people were both spiritually alive and puzzled. As Laubach talked to them, they said over and over that something had happened to them in that service that had never happened to them in church before.

On the way out of the church, Frank Laubach talked to the pastor and complimented him on his message. The pastor, who seemed a bit befuddled, said, "I don't understand it. I don't think I ever preached like that before. When I stepped into the pulpit, I felt more spiritually dry than I ever had before. But about five minutes into the sermon, I felt seized by God and I began to preach things that I had never planned to say. And it was wonderful!"

If one man can focus the Spirit on a preacher and resurrect him from the dead, can you imagine what would happen if a whole group of people joined together and gave themselves to that task? Can you imagine what could happen if all across this country groups of church members not only prayed *for* their pastors, but became channels through whom the Holy Spirit could flow *toward* pastors? Might not these pastors be empowered to be prophets? Might not revival begin in the households of God? Might this not be the beginning of the spiritual renewal that we need?

To the laity of the churches I make this plea. Would each of you ask some others in your church who crave revival to covenant with you to pray *for* your pastors, and would you commit yourselves to becoming channels through whom the Holy Spirit can empower them?

Pray for your pastor lovingly and in a spirit of support and encouragement, not critically or destructively. Does he bear burdens which you can help relieve? Can he count on your willingness to serve? Are you willing to roll up your sleeves and get stuck in alongside him?

Your pastor need not know about it. Tell him or her about your covenant to pray only if you think that the knowledge of what is going on would provide encouragement.

I long to hear of countless prayer vigils being held for pastors. And I can hardly wait to see the consequences of Christians sitting in congregations on Sunday mornings focusing the power of the Spirit, like laser beams, upon those who are preaching the word.

What They Didn't Teach Me at Bible College

It would help if our theological colleges trained pastors to do the things that make for revival. They could start by taking another look or two at what they are teaching candidates for the Christian ministry. If we are to have the kind of pastoral leadership that can motivate church members into the kinds of mid-range programmes that we need to affect communities, and if we are to have the kind of praxis among Christians that will give them a revived spirituality, we need the colleges to rethink their missions.

When, some thirty-five years ago, I announced to a friend of mine who was the pastor of a large African-American church that I was going to go to theological college, my black friend responded by asking, "What are you doing that for? By the time they finish with you at that place, you won't have enough power to preach the fuzz of a peach!"

There was much truth to that preacher's warning. Theological college did, in many ways, have a stifling effect on my enthusiasm for ministry. The studies in textual criticism, the rationalized theologies, and the courses in church management all had a tendency to socialize me into a religious bureaucrat who was ready to run an institution but was not very certain why he was doing it. What the sociologist Max Weber called the "routinization of Charisma" occurs in seminaries and causes some of us to wonder whether or not such institutions are good for the training of preachers. I have seen far too many seminarians lose "something" during their three years of training for me to leave these crucial institutions unscathed by any kind of critique.

In reflection, it may have been what the colleges did *not* teach me that irritates me more than anything else about them. In talking to others in the Christian ministry, I get a general opinion that their theological colleges left them unprepared to be effective in their calling. It is almost as though there were a need for a seminary equivalent of the best-selling book, *What They Didn't Teach Me at Harvard Business School*.

I have talked to a lot of ministers and have had an opportunity to reflect on my own experiences. The following is a list of some of the things that I wished I had learned during my days of ministerial training.

1. *I wish they had told me not to get involved in building programmes*. Somehow the clergy are easily seduced into what I call "the edifice complex". I know I certainly was. It is the idea that you are not really succeeding in ministry and your

church isn't really progressing unless you put up a new Christian education facility, or better still, a bigger sanctuary for worship.

Of course in Europe many church buildings are "listed". They have stood for centuries as the visible focal point of a parish, town or city. They consume vast amounts of money and time very often, and clergy are unwittingly cast in the role of architectural specialists, museum curators and fund-raisers.

I have found that all too often, building buildings kills the dynamic of churches and tends to divert the attention of the people from the real mission of Christianity. People often become so preoccupied with building-fund drives and with the colour of the new carpeting that they lose sight of their responsibility to minister to the needs of those who are hurting and to communicate the good news of God's love to those who need to be saved. I am sure that there are exceptions, but in more cases than not, building programmes use up a lot of money and energy that would better be used in outreach ministries to those in the outside world.

In America we have spent over $180 billion on church buildings to honour one who told us, "I dwell not in temples made with human hands." Think of what might have happened, not only to America but to the people in our churches, if that money, and the energy that goes with it, had been spent on the following:

- Building houses for the poor

- Sponsoring ministries for runaway teenagers

- Providing shelters for the homeless

- Setting up care centres for those with drug addictions

- Establishing halfway houses for prison inmates

- Carrying out local efforts to clean up the environment

- Providing medical and legal services for poor people

- Creating small businesses to provide employment for jobless people

- Setting up latchkey and tutoring programmes for socially disadvantaged children

- Providing help and services for single parents

- Undergirding efforts in minority communities to overcome the effects of racism and poverty

- Setting up care centres for battered women

- Developing both total care and day care for the elderly

- Developing AIDS hospices

- Providing counselling and an education fund for potential college students who come from poor backgrounds

- Promoting Christian arts

The list could go on and on. But more important than any and all of these is the question of what would have happened if that money and effort had been channelled into the kind of holistic evangelism that makes Jesus Christ real and meaningful to millions who only know about Him second hand.

I am not suggesting that there is never a need for church buildings and Christian education facilities. But in most instances there are alternatives. The cinema in town could be used for Sunday morning services; so could the banquet hall at a local hotel. There are schools that can be rented on weekends for Sunday School classes, as well as gyms and auditoriums that are available. The idea of spending piles of money for building space that is usually used for only a few hours a week seems like a bad one to me.

In theological college they never taught me about the hidden cost of a building programme. They never explained that if I organized my people to put up a sanctuary or a Christian education building, there would be little attention and few resources given to those mid-range programmes and projects that can make churches into transforming agents in their communities. They never made it clear that unless the church used its people and its wealth for the latter rather than the former, the church would be seen by those outside it as an institution that wanted to *use* them to pay off mortgages instead of as a group of self-sacrificing people who were responding to the needs of a hurting world.

2. *I wish they had told me that every church I served should really be seen as more than one congregation and that I should have different ministries for each of them.* In almost every church, first of all, there are the traditionalists. They are the ones who want the church to function only in forms with which they have always been familiar. Inexperienced pastors have a strong tendency to want to shake these "old fogies" out of their traditional moulds and *make* them experience new styles of worship and new dimensions of Christian mission. As a matter of fact, that is precisely what I came out of college thinking I was supposed to do.

If I had it to do over again, I wouldn't be so hard on these traditionalists. If they find worship more meaningful in their time-honoured forms, I would respect that and give them the Gospel in those old forms. If the established ways of carrying on ministry are the ones that they prefer, I could honour that.

It wouldn't have killed me to have paid a visit to the monthly meeting of the Ladies' Missionary Society. As a matter of fact, I might actually have enjoyed it. And the Annual Garden Party isn't some evil thing that must be set aside for something more "theologically relevant". The Garden Party just might be a good time to relax and meet people.

That visitation programme that the old deacons said would get me into every home of the families of the church each year is really not a bad idea. This is particularly true if the conversation moves beyond the small talk that often characterizes such visits and gets into the real joys and difficulties of living a spiritual life.

However, while I was doing all of these traditional things, I would also nurture another congregation in the church that had another vision of what the church should be and do. And in every church you can find them. These people could worship at an hour that differed from the traditional hour of worship. Their worship service, with all of its banners and contemporary music, might even take place on a Saturday night. There are some tremendous examples of this happening in the UK – the Nine o'Clock Service at Sheffield and Joy in Oxford to name but two. Traditionalists can be quite tolerant of alternative forms of worship as long as nobody *forces* them to share in it and if some respect is shown for what they like. The creative kinds of mid-range programmes and projects that I have been talking about can usually be started up with few problems as long as I don't disturb what the traditionalists have always been doing. A great deal of innovation can take place without making traditionalists unhappy.

If I didn't have enough of "my own" people for such new approaches to ministry and service, I would work ecumenically. There undoubtedly would be other churches with other pastors who have the same kind of hunger for innovation and daring.

There are three relatively small churches I know about that each week have one shared creative worship service together. The pastors and the people who share in this creative ecumenical worship service chip in to pay the salary of a special minister who leads a youth programme involving teenagers from all three of the churches. These pastors are beginning to get people together to build housing for the poor in the community, and they are also developing a shared ministry that is getting their people involved with an inner-city tutoring programme. All of this is happening without angering the traditionalists, who only want to worship on Sunday at eleven.

In theological college, I was taught that the ecumenical movement was always some theological thing that was supposed to lead to denominational mergers. They never told me that it was about networking creatively to develop the new kinds of ministries that communities need, and that a lot of people in the churches need if they are going to be alive in Christ.

Of course, when I suggest such things, ministers often cry that they just could never find the time to do all of these creative things and still keep the traditional programmes. I can just hear them complaining, "Those mid-range programmes that you are talking about are for people with time on their hands. I don't have the time to keep up with the things I have got to do now. All this talk about organizing people for community outreach programmes ignores my time limitations." That leads me to the third lesson left untaught in seminary.

3. *I wish they had taught me something about time management.* Most of the ministers I know end up immobilized and doing

very little in the course of a week. This is primarily because they just do not know how to organize time to get things done.

Many ministers fool others and themselves into believing that they do extensive reading and spend long hours in sermon preparation. Most of them don't. Most sermons are Saturday-night jobs – and it shows.

Ministers claim that they must attend endless meetings. And they may be half right. A good number of those meetings might not really be necessary. Too often, meetings are held for the sake of meeting. And worse than that, often very little planning goes into getting ready for church meetings. An agenda is seldom prepared ahead of time, and a schedule for issues to be discussed is rarely established. The result is that church meetings are usually the longest, dullest meetings any of us ever attend.

We ministers must learn to trust the laity. One reason ministers are so pressed for time is that they feel that they have to do everything themselves. Too often, ministers are on mini power trips and they are afraid to let anybody else in on the work of their churches for fear that they might have to let go some of that power. But if ministers in ordinary churches would turn over a lot of what they control to ordinary lay persons, they would have a lot more time to do a lot of extraordinary things.

4. *I wish they had taught me that I ought to spend most of my time in my home town.* It is so easy if you are in a mainline denomination to get sucked into denominational work and end up giving away too much time to what has no bearing on local ministry and the local church. I suppose denominational meetings are important for those who want to climb up the religious ladder of success. But I have a feeling that most of those who climb that ladder end up realizing

when they get to the top that the ladder was leaning against the wrong wall.

I myself have spent huge chunks of time going to denominational meetings that I now know were a waste of time. Long hours were spent hammering out watered-down resolutions that said almost nothing on such issues as abortion, homosexuality, and the Middle East, only to have those resolutions ignored by politicians and sometimes do little more than irritate people in the local congregations.

I fully realize that denominational youth conventions are of great value and that denominational mission work is usually the most progressive in vision and most cost-efficient. But denominational executives know what they are doing, and all of those powwows to get "input" from local pastors is more of an exercise in public relations than a good way of developing programmes. A lot of valuable time that is needed on the local level gets wasted.

Ministers must learn to stay put. Local initiatives gain wide support only if community people are convinced the ministers who are inspiring them to action are there for the long haul. Time and time again I have to listen to young ministers who are just out of theological college complain about the reluctance of their congregations to get moving on any of their grand schemes. "Why should they?" I ask myself. After all, those people are not fools. They know that the ambitious young preacher with the "big ideas" is going to be moving on to "bigger and better things" in just a short time, leaving them holding the baby. I know because I was once one of those brash young ministers. The fact that churches survive the likes of me is sufficient testimony to the grace of God.

Over the last fifteen years, my co-workers and I have been working with community people in several low-cost government housing projects in the run-down sections of Philadelphia. What my team of workers has pulled off is a justifiable source of the right kind of pride. They have made the kind of mid-range programmes that I have been telling you about really work. But the success of the Evangelical Association for the Promotion of Education has been largely due to its staying power.

The first few years we were engaged in ministry, we gained very little community support. We were, at best, tolerated. The people of these communities had seen social workers and community organizers come and go. They had become sceptical about the big talk, about the big plans, that such people brought with them. When we came along, we were put in the same category as that long line of "do-gooders" who had marched through these people's communities. It took almost five years before they came to trust us. And they did not come to trust us until they were sure we were not going to go away. When we bought houses and moved into the community, they knew we were not carpetbaggers but rather people who wanted to belong. It was then that they accepted us and things began to happen.

During my days in theological college, I was fortunate enough to be a student assistant pastor with a senior minister who had his head screwed on right. His name is John David Burton. He is now retired from the full-time pastorate (though not from service to the Kingdom). That part of his ministry was confined to two communities – Mount Holly, New Jersey, where I worked with him, and Clarendon Hills, Illinois. When a preacher stays in towns as long as John David did, people learn to support the dreams and visions that are articulated from the pulpit. He showed me the kinds of things that a pastor is able to inspire if he or she stays put.

The other thing that John David taught me was how to use time. I had to be in the office at 8:00 in the morning, and I had to go from there into the community to carry out a list of responsibilities that had been carefully scheduled for me. What I was able to accomplish in Mount Holly, just working on weekends, astound me as I look back on those formative years. But I was able to do it because I worked with a man who had been in town long enough to know what had to be done and who made me use my time efficiently in getting it done. He regularly recited to me his favourite line: "The children of darkness are wiser than the children of light – and they work harder too! Let's turn that around."

I am fortunate to have worked with John David Burton. He taught me what I should have learned in seminary. If there were more John David Burtons around, the revival might already be further along.

Chapter 10

Even Till the End of This Age

As a boy growing up in America, the only reason I could figure out for wanting to be converted was so that I could go to Heaven when I died. Since I wasn't planning on dying in the near future the conversion thing had very little attraction for me. I maintained this indifference to conversion through most of my teenage years. And I did so in spite of the evangelists who visited my church and warned the likes of me that we were in mortal danger.

"You think nothing's going to happen to you because you're young," the evangelists would shout. "Well, you could walk out of this church tonight, be walking across the street, and get hit by a truck. Then where would you be? In Heaven? Or in Hell?"

That sort of threat never really got to me, although I must admit that it did make me more cautious about crossing streets.

But as I grew older, I discovered that something was missing from my life. I am sure you have heard that line before. It is usually the line that those who give their testimonies at religious gatherings can be counted on to give. The line has become a cliché. But like most clichés, it became one because it is true.

Most people reach a time when they become susceptible to what I call "the Peggy Lee syndrome" and say to themselves, "Is this all there is?" Like myself, they begin to look for some ultimate meaning to their lives. So it was that I began to ask why I was here.

Why was I me and not someone else? Was I just an accident, or did my life have some kind of purpose and plan? Questions like those began to haunt me.

My Calvinistic Calling

In my teenage years, I came under some solid Calvinistic teachings. The doctrines of John Calvin left me convinced tha God had a plan for my life and that being a Christian was not just believing in Jesus and what He had done for me on the cross but also involved committing myself to living out His plan for my life.

I did not have any specifics, but I knew His plan involved my participation with Him in trying to change the world into the kind of world He wants it to be. Whether it was preaching to win people to Christ so that they could be people of His Kingdom, teaching in the classroom to prepare young people to be agents of change, or engaging in direct action against the war in Vietnam or to save the environment, I always saw my calling as living out the Lord's Prayer. I always wanted to see the Kingdom come "on earth as it is in heaven".

I want to invite others to share in that commitment. It is my hope that Christian conversion will move beyond a salvation experience that results only in a personal piety that gets people ready for Heaven. Conversion must involve people in the affairs of *this* world. If there is to be a rebirth of the West, it will come only as we become engaged in those activities that affect society with the values of the Sermon on the Mount. That is why I have so strongly pled for Christians to become committed to living out their faith in mid-range programmes and projects designed to implement something of the agenda of the Kingdom of God.

In the praxis of trying to change the world, I found the meaning and psychic energy that comes from reflection in action. It was in *doing* Christianity in those places where I lived and worked that the significance of my life became clear.

I am committed to global concerns such as world hunger. As a matter of fact, I am very involved in raising money for hungry children in Third-World countries. But it is setting up feeding programmes for the homeless in my own community that has the greatest effect on me. I believe that something must be done to curtail the demolition of the rain forest in the Amazon lest our ecological balance be permanently disturbed. I sign petitions and write to politicians to voice my concerns. But it is activities like organizing people in my own backyard to stop the use of styrofoam cups in fast-food restaurants that gets my blood running hot and stirs me to meaningful excitement.

I believe in world peace, and I am anxious to support candidates for public office who are committed to non-military solutions to world problems. But it is the reconciling of white people and black people in my own city through their work together in our tutoring programme for inner-city youth that really gets me "turned on" and feeling alive.

I could go on, but I think you get the point. As important as the big issues are in the grand scheme of living on spaceship earth, it is my participation with mid-range activities wherein I am *directly* involved in what is happening and can see for myself the results of my efforts that gives my life the enlivening spirit that takes the numbness of my soul away.

It is out of my personal experiences in living out the culural mandate of Calvinism that I have come to *feel* that my life has significance. It is in trying to change the world on the local level that I have sensed personal purpose and meaning.

Recently I heard a recording of country singers the Statler

Brothers. The lyrics of one of their songs had a haunting, tragic quality. They went like this:

> Tommy's selling' used cars,
> Nancy's fixin' hair.
> Harvey runs a groc'ry store,
> And Margaret doesn't care.
> Jerry drives a truck for Sears
> And Charlotte's on the make
> And Paul sells life insurance
> And part-time real estate.
>
> And the class of '57 had its dreams.
> We all thought we'd change the world
> With out great works and deeds: Or
> Maybe we just thought the world
> Would change to fit our needs.
> The class of '57 had its dreams.
>
> Betty runs a trailer park,
> Jan sells Tupperware.
> Randy's in an insane ward
> And Mary's on welfare;
> Charley took a job with Ford,
> Joe took Freddy's wife.
> Charlotte took a millionaire
> and Freddy took his life.
>
> But the class of '57 had its dreams
> Ah, the class of '57 had its dreams.

Such are the tragedies of people who do not recognize that dreams can be lived out and purposes realized right where we live in our everyday lives. That is one reason why these mid-range programmes and projects of which I have been speaking are so important.

A Touch of the Charismatic

In the mid-seventies I got my first strong dose of the charismatic movement, and I liked it. Earlier in my life I had experienced brief brushes with this dynamic expression of Christianity, but it was not until I started preaching in Pentecostal churches and at various "Jesus festivals" that I began to grasp the importance of what was happening through the charismatic movement.

At first I was turned off by the emphasis that those in the charismatic movement put on "praying in tongues". I did not understand it, nor did I have any desire to get into it. It was only gradually that I came to realize that the "tongues thing" was only one small part of what the charismatic movement was all about, and became open to what it could offer me.

What happened at the worship services at charismatic gatherings gave me the best understanding of the significance of this movement. Time and time again, I sensed a "power" or a "presence" come upon me in the spontaneity of charismatic worship. On many of these occasions I felt as though I had experienced some special kind of inner release. Excitement and joy filled me, and I hungered to have these experiences more often.

At the Creation Festival, a kind of religious Woodstock that is held each year in central Pennsylvania, I experienced something of the charismatic movement without the tongues experience. The Creation Festival brings together forty thousand Christians each year for four days of contemporary Christian music and intensive preaching. Since Harry Thomas, the sponsor and promoter of the festival, is a former student of mine, I can always count on being invited to be one of the speakers.

Just before going on stage during the 1979 festival, I sensed something extra special. It was something new to me. There was a "filling of the Spirit". Call it the result of the "collective effervescence" of the crowd, as the sociologist Emile Durkheim would, or call it some kind of "psychological high" generated by the intensity of the situation. All I know is that I felt a presence. An exhilaration ran through my being, and I was lifted to a very special state of ecstasy. It has been easy ever since that experience to relate to what the seventeenth-century philosopher and scientist Blaise Pascal experienced when he wrote:

> From about half past ten in the evening
> to about a half hour after midnight –
> *FIRE!*
> God of Abraham, God of Isaac, God of Jacob,
> Not the God of philosophers and scholars,
> Absolute Certainty; Beyond Reason,
> Joy, Peace.
> Forgetfulness of the world and everything
> but God.
> The world has not known thee
> But I have known thee.
> Joy! Joy! Joy! Tears of Joy!

My experience also had, in my mind, a certain kinship to what John Wesley described about his Aldersgate experience:

In the evening I went very unwillingly to a society in Aldersgate Street, where one was reading Luther's *Preface to the Epistle to the Romans*. About a quarter before nine, while he was describing the change which God works in the heart through faith in Christ, I felt my heart strangely warmed. I felt that I did trust in Christ, Christ alone for salvation; and an assurance was given me, that he had taken away my sins, even mine, and saved me from the law of sin and death. I began to pray with all my might for those who had in a more especial manner dispitefully used me and persecuted me. I then testified openly to all there what I now first felt in my heart.

This kind of experience was the charismatic movement in a form that I could embrace. And I did!

All across the United States, charismatic churches are growing by leaps and bounds. Charismatic Christianity is the fastest-growing form of Christianity around. More and more of those who join these churches are doing so without ever speaking or praying in tongues. It is the *worship* that attracts them. They are tired of the traditional worship of mainline denominational Christianity. People are lured into the charismatic movement because the worship services give them a feeling of having been released from the weight of guilt and anxiety that so often go with living in our kind of world. All the emotions that our consumer-oriented society promises to deliver if we will just buy its things are more than experienced in a full surrender to the Holy Spirit.

Consumerism may actually have helped to bring on the charismatic experiences that are increasingly evident throughout Christendom. The things that have been advertised to us with the promise that they can deliver certain emotional gratifications have failed to do so. But as an unintended side effect the ads have made us more aware of what is missing in our lives and have stimulated the hunger to have these emotional and spiritual needs met. In a sense, I believe that the manipulations of the media on behalf of consumerism have been the John the Baptist that has prepared the way for the charismatic movement. It is no wonder that so many are becoming neo-Pentecostal. In the worship of the charismatic movement, people are finding that which the consumeristic ads have promised but never have given.

There is an old hymn entitled "Spirit of the Living God" that describes what people are looking for in the charismatic movement. It tells of something more profound than the often sensational demonstrations of the outpouring of Spirit that are represented by praying in tongues or in healing services. Instead, this hymn speaks of taking away the dimness of the soul and of the craving for inner renewal:

> I ask no dream, no prophet's ecstasies,
> No sudden rending of the veil of clay;
> No angel visitant, no opening skies,
> But take the dimness of my soul away.

This kind of mystical dimension to religious experience is part of the coming revival that I believe offers hope for the Western world, numbed as it is by consumeristic values.

I would be amiss if I did not point out that spiritual renewal is also being found through means other than the charismatic movement. There is a new interest in the kind of contemplation advocated by the likes of Thomas Merton, author of *The Seven Storey Mountain* and *Seeds of Contemplation*.* This too has played a part in generating the kind of spiritual renewal that breaks the bonds of psychic deadness that had come to mark our culture. It is true that there are other ways in which people are beginning to experience the revitalization of the spirit that can save the West. I speak so strongly of the charismatic movement only

---

*Thomas Merton, *The Seven Storey Mountain*, New York: Harcourt, Brace, 1948; *Seeds of Contemplation*, New York: Farrar, Straus, Giroux, 1964.

because it is the most evident of the renewal instruments of our time and is obviously affecting the most people.

Add a Little of the Anabaptist Lifestyle

Ron Sider, author of *Rich Christians in an Age of Hunger*,* teaches at Eastern Baptist Theological Seminary, a sister school to Eastern College, where I teach. We are friends who interact with fair regularity. Consequently, I have been influenced by his countercultural Anabaptist theology. At a time when I felt a need for an alternative to the dominant values and lifestyle of our consumer-oriented society, his views proved most attractive and helpful.

In America the Anabaptists have both a realism and a humility that keeps them from the triumphalism that has marked many evangelicals of the last decade. They are well aware that there are demonic forces everywhere that are not about to beat a retreat just because some zealous youth speaker calls upon those in the audience to "take over the world for Jesus". They know all too well that our society is not going to show much evidence of becoming the Kingdom of God without God Himself dramatically intervening in history.

On the other hand, Anabaptists believe that Christians are supposed to "set up" that Kingdom in the midst of this world as a kind of alternative to what is offered by the dominant "Kingdoms of this world".

The primary spokespersons for Anabaptist theology, who include Donald Kraybill, Ron Sider, and John Howard Yoder, are being heard by Christians from groups as far-ranging and different from one another as the liberal National Council of

---

*Ron Sider, *Rich Christians in an Age of Hunger*, Downers Grove, IL: Inter-Varsity, 1984.

Churches and the fundamentalist National Association of Evangelicals. Their books have become best-sellers, and their influence is conditioning the way the rest of us Christians look at the world.

Those in this Anabaptist tradition have not given up on the world. Instead, they have a different methodology for trying to change it. They contend that the most important task for Christians is to establish communities that reveal to the rest of the world the kind of society that God wants to establish here on earth. Often referred to as the Radical Reformation, they promote a lifestyle in community that literally adheres to the teachings of Jesus. Anabaptists are committed pacifists, zealous in ministering to the poor, and self-sacrificing servants to the oppressed and beaten down people of the world. The relief organizations of Anabaptist denominations maintain some of the most extensive and effective social service programmes and economic development efforts of Christendom. They are dedicated to what they call "the servant ministries" of Jesus.

I was in a Mennonite church the Sunday after a major earthquake hit Mexico City. The pastor announced that ten members of the congregation would be leaving that very day to go to Mexico City to serve as relief workers and that they would stay for at least a month to help the victims of the earthquake rebuild. Other members of the church were expected to fill in for these relief workers on their regular jobs, take care of the families that they left behind, and help to cover all the expenses they incurred by being away from their homes.

This incredible capacity for mobilization to meet a crisis in Mexico is just one of hundreds of ways that Anabaptists are ready to serve the world. This service is rendered in love. It is not an attempt to gain control over the social system nor is it meant to be a means of gaining political power. As a matter of fact, strict adherence to their beliefs would keep them from holding political office, being on the police force, and even voting. They want not to take over the world but to change it through loving service. They want to affect the world through what they *are* as well as what they *do*.

To use an illustration taken from the Harvard theologian Harvey Cox, Anabaptists are attempting to become God's Nova Huta. Cox explains that when the communists took over in Poland following World War II, they established what they thought would be the perfect communist city. This city, called Nova Huta, was to have ideal housing and the best possible parks and recreational facilities. It was to have excellent schools and to provide near-to-ideal work conditions. Only people who were ideologically pure communists were allowed to be citizens of Nova Huta.

The idea behind the creation of this city was that it be a demonstration of the future of Poland, set down in the midst of the present. Nova Huta was to be a sermon to the rest of Poland about what communism was attempting to create for everyone in the nation. Its primary function was to *be* all that communism was supposedly able to make a city to be. The very existence of Nova Huta was supposed to help convert the rest of Poland to a new way of life.

Anabaptists, in their traditional form, seek to do much the same thing. They want to affect the world by what they *are*. They want their lives-in-community to be so attractive that people will want to leave the ways of the world and live in accord with the will of God. They hope that the values of the Kingdom of God that they live out in their everyday lives will be so validated in the eyes of the world that those who govern its societies will endeavour to implement these values within their spheres of influence.

However, Anabaptists do not kid themselves into believing that there is no need for the Second Coming of Christ. They

are convinced that while the world may be affected by the
presence of communities of radically committed Christians,
it will take an invasion from beyond society and from outside
history to purge the world of sin and to create the Kingdom
of God on earth.

As an illustration of what is hoped for, let me tell you about
the role of the French underground movement during World
War II. The brave men and women in that movement were
well aware of their limitations as they challenged their Nazi
conquerors. They knew that they alone could not overthrow
their oppressors. But in the backs of their minds, they had
hope. It was a hope that a huge invasion force was being
gathered across the English Channel. Furthermore, they were
convinced that, in an hour none of them knew, an invasion
force would sweep onto the shores of France and join up with
their ragtag army and carry them to victory. The underground
movement believed that when that great day came, all that
they had worked and suffered to achieve would be given new
and wonderful significance. They were convinced that, in that
hour, they would know that their labour had not been in
vain.

In a parallel fashion, Anabaptist Christians see themselves
as a kind of underground movement for God. They struggle
against an awesome enemy and seem to be up against
insurmountable odds. But in their efforts to bring in the
Kingdom of God, they labour with hope. They believe that,
in an hour known only to the Heavenly Father, their Christ
will re-enter human history and bring to realization the world
they have been trying to create. They know that what they
do in the way of social ministry is a sign of this coming event.
And they believe that none of their efforts to build a Kingdom
will have been in vain.

Linking Anabaptist Theology with Mid-Range Social Change

It is easy to see how such a theology can be integrated with the kind of mid-range projects that we have been talking about. Small community-based programmes designed to give expression to the values of the Kingdom of God as expressed in Scripture can have ultimate significance within this vision. Christian activists do not necessarily have to see the whole world change. It is enough for them to realize some small sign or evidence of the Kingdom in the projects they have taken into hand. They do not have to see Satan flee or evil disappear. It is enough for them to know that the good that they do will not be lost and that when the Lord returns, the Evil One and all of his works will be destroyed. Within the context of this optimistic view of history, there is the assurance that, though the cause of evil may prosper, it cannot retard or extinguish the work of God's people. In all of this, Anabaptists and other Christian activists agree.

Labouring to set up a feeding programme for children in Haiti will not solve all the hunger problems of that country. But Christ will honour that effort and complete what it was intended to accomplish when He returns.

Building houses for poor people through Habitat for Humanity will not eliminate slums from the face of the earth. But those who build these houses can do so in the assurance that Christ will receive their hard work and, on the day of His coming, expand it into something that provides dignified living conditions for everyone.

Working to get a citywide ruling outlawing styrofoam cups at fast-food chains will not end the pollution of the environment nor do away with the impending ecological holocaust. But those who engage in such limited social action projects can look forward to a day when the Lord of History will make all things new.

Starting small businesses in Third-World countries will not bring an end to poverty. But those who believe in His impending coming can do so knowing that what they do is the beginning of the end of a world of privation for some of God's children.

It is not simply that God will do something *alongside* these community-based micro projects. If that were the case, these efforts would be rendered insignificant at the Second Coming of Christ. Rather, God will take what His people have initiated and explode it into the fulfilment of His will for the world. Jesus says that such small and seemingly insignificant projects are actually *seeds* out of which will come the full-grown manifestation of the Kingdom of God.

My religious journey is not unusual. I am finding that people everywhere are coming to this same kind of Christianity. The countervailing influences of a Calvinism that takes changing the world as a mandate, a Pentecostalism that finds spontaneity and joy in worship, and an Anapbaptist awareness that the best we can hope to achieve before "the end" is to establish "islands of Kingdom" where the ethic of the Kingdom can be lived out all come together to form a new version of holistic Christianity. I believe that these three religious commitments and experiences, properly synthesized, are the hope of the future. Together, I believe, they will create an enlivened people who, in their living out of the Gospel in mid-range ways, will give new birth to a dying nation.

A Harvest for the World

Across the West and around the world, the seeds have been sown that even now are beginning to come to fruition in a new breed of radical Christians. No-one seems to be able to name the prophet who sowed these seeds, but that they *have been sown* is hard to deny.

The future is hard to figure out. We know that these seeds of repentance and renewal will fall on different kinds of soil. Some who receive these seeds will be superficial in their commitment and, lacking depth, will turn away from this radical Christianity. They will discard it, as bohemians eventually turn from old fads and look for something new.

Others will find the going too tough. They will be those who really did not count the cost of this kind of discipleship before they got started (Luke 14:25–33). They will give up and look for easier ways to live.

Still others will be seduced back into the ways of the world. After all, the sensuous allurements of the things of Babylon are more than most of us can resist. With the TV ads packaging things in erotic and egotistic wrappers, it is hard to resist buying. Before they know it, some people will be sucked back in. Instead of being committed to the justice of the Kingdom, they will be worried once again about how they can hold onto the things that they have acquired and will be concerned about how they can get more.

But every so often, and more often than one might think, there will be those individuals who get a handle on the message, realize what is involved, and go with it all the way. As the prophetic seeds take root in them, they will seek to do the works of righteousness (Matthew 5:6). In dark and forgotten places they will try to do what must be done for justice to roll down and for *shalom* to thrive. What they try to accomplish will often leave them frustrated, but they will learn from their frustrations. The people they try to serve will hurt them many times, but they will learn to see Jesus in these people anyway. What they achieve will be limited in the world's eyes, but they *will* learn how to overcome the world (John 16:33). And in the end they will bear fruit. Eventually their efforts will come to greatness. Even the seemingly little things that they do will have their rewards (Matthew 10:42). And when these people come together, they will be a presence that the world will not be able to ignore. They will be a new people who will shake the foundations of the old order. They will be a leaven in society. They will be the salt of the earth. They will be the beginning of a new Kingdom, even as the old world passes away.

And Jesus said:

Behold, a sower went forth to sow;
   And when he sowed, some seeds fell by the way side, and the fowls came and devoured them up;
   Some fell upon stony places, where they had not much earth; and forthwith they sprung up, because they had no deepness of earth;
   And when the sun was up, they were scorched; and because they had no root, they withered away.
   And some fell among thorns; and the thorns sprung up, and choked them:
   But other fell into good ground, and brought forth fruit, some an hundredfold, some sixtyfold, some thirtyfold.
   Who hath ears to hear, let him hear.

Matthew 13:3–9

I am filled with hope because there is good seed in the world. That seed has taken root and it will not be long before it yields a harvest that will bless us all.